BOLINGBROKE AND FRANCE

Rex A. Barrell

UNIVERSITY
PRESS OF
AMERICA

Lanham • New York • London

1988

Copyright © 1988 by

University Press of America,® Inc.

4720 Boston Way
Lanham, MD 20706

3 Henrietta Street
London WC2E 8LU England

British Cataloging in Publication Information Available

Library of Congress Cataloging-in-Publication Data

Barrell, Rex A.
Bolingbroke and France / by Rex A. Barrell.
p. cm.
Bibliography: p.
Includes index.
1. Bolingbroke, Henry St. John, Viscount, 1678–1751—Homes and
haunts—France. 2. Bolingbroke, Henry St. John, Viscount,
1678–1751—Views on France. 3. Bolingbroke, Henry St. John,
Viscount, 1678–1751—Influence. 4. Politicians—Great Britain—
Biography. 5. France—Intellectual life—18th century. 6. Great
Britain—Intellectual life—18th century. I. Title.
DA501.B6B33   1988
942.06'9'0924—dc 19   [B]   88–19852 CIP
ISBN 0–8191–7127–1 (alk. paper)

DEDICATION

TO   ROSALIND

AND

LLOYD

Henry St. John, Viscount Bolingbroke

Portrait by A. S. Belle

CONTENTS

PREFACE

Since planning this third part of the trilogy upon which I embarked several years ago (Chesterfield and Walpole having been published in 1968, and 1978-79), I discovered that Bolingbroke research was very active indeed, and that I was not the first in the field of Bolingbroke's relations with France.

However, as I had been granted leave and a Canada Council Fellowship to carry out this particular project, I decided to press on, while limiting the scope of my study to allow the definitive work to be published by a scholar whose credentials and ability are of the highest order.

I fully acknowledge my debt to Professor Dennis Fletcher of the University of Durham whose magisterial thesis on Bolingbroke's intellectual relations with France, as well as his articles in the same field, have been an invaluable aid. Professor Dickinson's standard biography of Bolingbroke, Professor Rousseau's monumental volumes on Voltaire and England, Professor Varey's recent studies of Bolingbroke, and Dr. Brean Hammond's perceptive account of Pope and Bolingbroke have also been of great assistance. Other names too numerous to mention here will be found in the bibliography.

All these works are ample proof that the reputation of Bolingbroke as a philosopher, a politician and an historian is still sufficiently high to attract interest over two hundred years after his death. An important part of this monograph is the conclusion where a sample of critical opinion on both sides of the Channel and even in America shows the continuing attention given to one of the eighteenth century's most fascinating and enigmatic personalities.

In this study all dates are given in the New Style (Gregorian Calendar). Special thanks are due to Mr. J. M. Armstrong, my research assistant at the Institute of Historical Research in London, Professors Conlon of McMaster University, Dickinson of Edinburgh University, Fletcher of Durham University, A-M Rousseau of Aix-Marseille, Varey of U.C.L.A., Doctors Brean Hammond of Liverpool and George Nadel of Horsham, Sussex for kind advice and helpful suggestions, Mr. Garth McCavana of McMaster University for analyzing Voltaire's correspondence, Madame

Mireille Zanuttini of Paris for checking French archives, Mrs. Patricia Gill, archivist of Chichester for listing pertinent MSS, Professor Stuart Hunter of the English Department at the University of Guelph, for his kindness and expertise in preparing the manuscript for publication and Miss Darlene Schooley, former secretary of the Department of Languages and Literatures at the University of Guelph, for her competent typing services. The Library staff of the University of Guelph are to be congratulated for their willing and tireless assistance in tracking down bibliographic sources and organizing inter-library loans. I am grateful also to the National Portrait Gallery of London for allowing me to use Belle's portrait of Bolingbroke and to the Canada Council for awarding me a fellowship to complete this study.

R.A. Barrell
University of Guelph
1988

INTRODUCTION

Of the important figures in England during the closing years of the seventeenth and much of the eighteenth century, three were undoubtedly the most significant as active intermediaries between France and their own country. These were, in chronological order: Bolingbroke, Chesterfield and Horace Walpole. Bolingbroke and Chesterfield were pre-eminent statesmen endowed in addition with all the social graces; Walpole dabbled in politics but had no wish or propensity to follow in his famous father's footsteps. He was, par excellence, a letter writer, a gazetteer who delighted to record for posterity all the political and social intrigues of his time, though at the same time he was an important literary figure, and a wide-awake critic who took great pains to pass judgment on each literary work of significance which appeared on both sides of the channel. Chesterfield too was a first class letter writer who, though the scope of his epistolary efforts was much more limited than Walpole's, took pleasure in commenting on literary works and political movements in both countries. Bolingbroke's correspondence, scattered throughout the world, is concerned more with philosophy, history and politics than with literary criticism or social trivia. All three were acquainted but what different types they were! Bolingbroke, brilliant, charming, mercurial, indiscreet; Chesterfield urbane, diplomatic, irreproachable; Walpole suave, ebullient, sly yet intensely humane. Bolingbroke was one of Chesterfield's idols, yet he regretted the dissipation of his private life and the waste of his talents; Walpole, moving in the shadow of his father, detested both Chesterfield and Bolingbroke mainly for their political beliefs. Three men of giant stature and fascinating interest, proved by the numerous studies that have been published from their deaths to the present day. Bolingbroke's works were reprinted in 1969 while his correspondence is being collated and edited by Simon Varey; Lewis's monumental edition of Walpole's correspondence has recently been completed; a new edition of Chesterfield's correspondence is in the capable hands of Cecil Price of Swansea. All three have been grossly maligned since their deaths, Chesterfield principally for the equivocal morality of his famous _Letters_, Walpole for

1

dilettantism, apparent lack of manliness, and his Frenchified dandyism (Wordsworth), Bolingbroke for his personal immorality and betrayal of friends and country. Saner heads now prevail, and a proper balance between faults and merits has been achieved (see Lewis's numerous studies of Walpole, Dickinson's standard work on Bolingbroke, and Mellor's fine book on Chesterfield). The greatest figure in eighteenth century France, Voltaire, was a friend and correspondent of all three men. He had stayed with Bolingbroke at La Source in France, been the guest of Chesterfield in London, and measured arms with Walpole. This monograph is firstly a chronological account of Bolingbroke's francophilic interests and activities, and secondly an investigation of the impact of his ideas (philosophical, historical and political) on French thought, and the debt that he owed to French writers. His familiarity with the latter is evidenced from reading his works and correspondence. Of these, Montaigne, Bayle, Descartes, Malebranche, and Rapin de Thoyras have pride of place.

PART I

BOLINGBROKE'S LIFE

Early Years

Born on 16 September 1678 at Lydiard Tregoze, the family seat in Wiltshire, Bolingbroke was later christened at Battersea, the home of his paternal grandparents, remaining there until his father remarried in 1687. Being a sickly child, he was sent for his education, probably not to Eton or Christ Church, but to a Dissenting Academy where the programs were not as rigorous. It is likely that his grandmother, Lady Johanna St. John, who took a considerable interest in his education, employed a Dissenting tutor, one Daniel Burgess. His stepmother, Angelica Magdalena Wharton, née Pellissary, came from a French-Swiss Huguenot family and would certainly have favored the idea of a Dissenting Academy to keep her strong links with the Huguenots in London. Her connections with the French salons of the Maréchal de Torcy, the Maréchal d'Huxelles and the court of the Maréchal de Berwick at Paris and Clermont were very important for her stepson in later life. Records are sparse for this early period of Bolingbroke's life, but it seems likely that the Academy he attended was Sheriffhales in Shropshire, which would have fostered his interest in languages, science, and civil law. His early mastery of the French language could have been the result of the efforts of both his step-mother and his languages tutor at the Academy. His step-sister Henrietta Howard, with whom Bolingbroke had a lifelong bond of affection, had a French governess, a certain Mlle Haillé, often mentioned in his correspondence with her.

During these early years Bolingbroke gained a reputation as a brilliant and sparkling conversationalist and public speaker, but also as a young rake who squandered his money on street-girls and ladies of easy virtue. In addition he shared the common aristocratic vice of over-indulgence in alcohol and may well have been the first streaker. Goldsmith reports him running naked across St. James Park in a fit of intoxication. There was always, however, a serious side to his nature. His sympathy for the Huguenots exiled to England after the Revocation of the Edict of Nantes, and for the plight of the English Protestants in France was very real, and he

3

contributed sums of money to their cause. Later, however, when he was attempting to bring about peace with France, their importunings and hostility towards any such move proved a considerable embarrassment. His idol at this stage of his life was Sir William Trumbull, the Tory Secretary of State who had not only avidly espoused the cause of the Huguenots, but attempted, when he was later ambassador in Paris, to ameliorate the situation of English Protestants in France. The favorite venue of both Huguenots and supporters in London was the famed Rainbow Coffee House where intellectual discussions on the evils of French despotism and the virtues of English democracy were the order of the day, a far cry from the rough atmosphere of other political clubs in England. It appears also that certain French refugees brought into the coffee house scene some of the literary activities so widespread in French salons of the time. Bolingbroke must surely have been a constant visitor, and his penchant for writing and declaiming pretty verses probably received considerable stimulus from such beaux esprits as Thémiseul de Saint-Hyacinthe. Here too Rapin de Thoyras gained his mastery of the English political system, and was later to popularise it in France in his great study, Histoire d'Angleterre, and indeed many English writers, including Bolingbroke himself, were indebted to Rapin's clear exposition in their own works.

Grand Tour

The Grand Tour, a voyage to the sources of humanist learning which Bolingbroke undertook between 1697 and 1699, was an essential feature of every young aristocrat's education, but unlike the copious reports of Chesterfield and Walpole when their turn came, little is recorded of his activities. What there is appears in his correspondence with Trumbull and the memoirs of his tour companion Edward Hopkins. No social, literary or picturesque accounts as flowed from the pen of Walpole and Chesterfield, but quite indignant comments on religious oppression and royal despotism, and comparisons between the situation in France and in England where liberty, tolerance and a limited monarchy were beneficial to all levels of society[1]. It is interesting to recall Chesterfield's remarks on the Pope ('un vieux fourbe') with Bolingbroke's on the superstitious and ignorant follies of the papal court and attendant friars, as well as his (and Walpole's) belief that the English constitution was the most perfect ever devised. Young

4

Voltaire was only a child of four at the time of this visit, but how similar he would be later to this brash, passionate, anti-clerical and iconoclastic hothead! Pleasure parties there were aplenty in the cities of France and Italy, but also serious comments on the state of learning in these countries, showing him to be, as Fletcher puts it, "a conscientious citizen of the Republic of letters"[2]. He has obviously read the exiled Saint-Evremond whom he cites in a letter to Trumbull of September 10, 1699, an alter ego in the sense that both were concerned with history, the historical process, and various philosophical subjects such as the nature of God and of human reason. No doubt Saint-Evremond's relaxed moral code (his rule for conquering passions was to indulge them) appealed greatly to the English _libertin_ as did his sceptical and epicurean temperament. A dilettante par excellence, he was Walpole's favorite philosopher, while his good breeding, graceful wit, and exquisite urbanity caused Chesterfield to sing his praises. Daniels was of Saintsbury's opinion that the latter was "le Saint-Evremond de l'Angleterre", and tried to prove that Bolingbroke was his intellectual successor[3]. It is likely also that at this stage of his life he was reading Pierre Bayle whose name occurs frequently in his works. Was it his mentor Trumbull who introduced Bayle to Bolingbroke? It is possible because Trumbull knew Bayle and had received a copy of the _Dictionary_ from him personally. However it may be, Bolingbroke's interest in a writer from whom the _philosophes_ would draw many of their weapons was hardly surprising. His rationalistic views and his critical approach to history, philosophy and chiefly religion were becoming widely known on both sides of the Channel. The famed _Dictionnaire historique et critique_ had appeared the same year as Bolingbroke's departure for Europe (1697), and he would surely have heard the work discussed in the salons and the intellectual coteries which he frequented. In Rome he frequented a group of _beaux esprits_ called the _Arcadia_ which used to meet on summer holidays in some garden to read and listen to extracts from literary works[4]. As a result of this tour, Bolingbroke acquired such a knowledge of the French language as to enable him to write and speak it with perfect ease, an accomplishment which was to be most valuable to him in his subsequent political career. Apparently he was the only one of the ministers who was able to negotiate with the French in their own language.

Political Office

Back in England in 1699, Bolingbroke seems to have renewed his poetical activities. He had earlier on composed some verses as a preface to Dryden's translation of the Aeneid, and these were afterwards prefixed, with some alterations, to a work of Saint-Hyacinthe published in Holland in 1714, le Chef d'oeuvre d'un inconnu. An ode published in 1700, Almahide, which had as its point de départ his resentment at the infidelity of a mistress, already gives some indication of the philosophical direction in which his mind was turning. In 1700 he married Frances Winchcombe, an heiress with estates in Berkshire, and shortly after (Feb. 1701) entered Parliament as a member for Wootton Bassett, in Wiltshire. His debut was even more brilliant than that of Chesterfield some years later.

The next fifteen years spent in office (except for 1708-10 when he was in virtual retirement) first as Secretary at War (1704), when he worked closely with another of his idols, the Duke of Marlborough, and then as Secretary of State (1710) when he reached his zenith as a politician and statesman, have been well documented and are not directly related to this study. However, a few highlights can be selected to show his varied interests. Even while immersed in business or given over to pleasure and hunting, Bolingbroke (who acquired his title of Viscount only in 1712) never ceased to pursue a well-oriented program of reading and studying; we do not know exactly what books he used, but we can be certain that his philosophical ideas were taking shape. Though happy leading the lonely life of a studious intellectual, he had to come out of retirement to engage in lively discussions with many different types of people -- philosophers, scientists, men of letters. And in this area Bolingbroke really shone; a sharp wit, a logical train of thought, a persuasive and eloquent discourse linked with his fine bearing and charismatic personality dazzled and influenced all with whom he came into contact. He was the founder of the famed Brothers' Club (1711) which developed from informal gatherings at the house of Robert Harley (later Earl of Oxford), another of his early idols. Though the Club rivalled the better known Kit-Kat Club, it had a far different orientation. Men of influence and power in the political world rubbed shoulders with wits and scholars, and the tone was much higher; there intellectual conversation, commentaries on and discussion of problems of everyday political life were the order of the day. A similar club founded in the early part of 1712 was the Political Academy of the Marquis de Torcy at the Louvre, mentioned in several of the periodicals of the day,[5] a sort of seminary for the training of future politicians. Torcy, nephew of Colbert and Secretary of State for Foreign Affairs from 1696 to 1715, maintained a regular correspondence with Bolingbroke on matters concerning the forthcoming Peace of Utrecht. It is not known whether Bolingbroke ever attended this academy, though in his correspondence with Trumbull he often fulminated against the notion of divine right of Kings, praising the English system of constitutional monarchy. The Abbé Gaultier, who had long lived in London as chaplain to foreign ministers and had become in some sort a French political agent, had taken the first steps in the peace proposals. In France at the end of 1710, he returned there in August of 1712 with Matthew Prior and Bolingbroke himself, the latter replacing the original negotiator, Lord Jersey. Prior, a poet as well as a diplomat and a great friend of Bolingbroke, remained in Paris after Bolingbroke's return, acting as a sort of intermediary keeping Bolingbroke in touch with activities and friends in France.

Three French Visits

Bolingbroke's reputation as a skillful negotiator and a polished diplomat had preceded him, and he received a royal welcome in France. Right from the landing at Calais cheering throngs surrounded him and lined the route to Paris itself. His crowded schedule in Paris included the treaty negotiations with Torcy who was his host at the Hôtel de Croissi, an interview with Louis XIV at Fontainebleau where he presented a letter from Queen Anne, and the normal round of receptions and pleasure parties[6]. Bolingbroke was greatly flattered by all the attentions and favors lavished upon him by the Torcy household, and after his return, kept up the friendship with Mme de Torcy and the Marquise de Croissi, Torcy's mother, sending them many gifts[7]. The friendship between Torcy and Bolingbroke was a cordial one based on common political interests, but once the Treaty was signed there was little further communication between them. There is no evidence for example of further contacts with the Hôtel de Croissi during Bolingbroke's future exile. During this visit, Bolingbroke, ever the charming rake, apparently enjoyed the favors of several of Paris' fascinating but uninhibited hostesses[8]. However, he was much more closely involved with Mme de Ferriol (née Guérin), whom he may have met during his <u>Grand Tour</u>[9], and who was to become one of his most faithful correspondents. She was the sister of the much better known, though notorious Abbé (later Cardinal) de Tencin and Mme Claudine de Tencin. It seems likely that he met both Mme de Ferriol and her brother during this visit but not the willful and passionate defrocked nun Claudine[10], with whom he was to be involved later. Fletcher notes[11] that most of Bolingbroke's biographers believed that Claudine had extracted diplomatic secrets from Bolingbroke, very likely during the ardor of a romantic tryst, but there is no evidence of this and Bolingbroke's standard biographer ignores it[12]. Chesterfield, much more circumspect than Bolingbroke, was a dispassionate admirer of Claudine whose salon he attended in 1741 and with whom he corresponded. On the vexed question of Bolingbroke's incipient involvement in the Jacobite intrigues of 1710-14, there is no evidence to support the claim that he met clandestinely with the Pretender during this visit. He did however attract criticism by attending the opera the very night of the Pretender's visit and may perhaps have greeted him in company with other notables.

Bolingbroke returned to England after his two week stay in Paris on August 28, 1712, travelling via Dunkirk. His reception in London was the exact opposite of that which he had received in Paris. Oxford, clearly jealous of Bolingbroke's success, accused him of political machinations and machiavellianism, exceeding his instructions, and of gross misconduct bordering on treachery. Rumors of his indiscretions with Mme de Tencin and of his supposed private meeting with the Pretender had reached England before his return. This constant bickering led finally to an open breach with Oxford, and Bolingbroke saw his hopes for a top post in his party rudely shattered. In this situation as in others he was his own worst enemy. Arrogant, egotistical, and power-hungry, his equivocal moral and political conduct more than balanced his undoubted gifts as an eloquent and passionate envoy for his native country. And in a crisis Bolingbroke's self-assurance always abandoned him. The dismissal of Oxford and the death of Queen Anne, as well as warnings from friends and enemies alike that his political future and even his life were in jeopardy, put him in a state of constant trepidation where his judgment became completely clouded[13]. He could have ridden out the storm by remaining in England and asserting his innocence, if innocent he was, but he chose to flee, always a sign of fear stemming from guilt. Even if he was too proud and sensitive to beg for clemency from a despised Tory party or for mercy from a vengeful Whig majority, he could have retired from politics to a quiet, studious, rustic life. Overweening ambition however and a driven sense of his own destiny obfuscated any transient yearnings for a change of life. He was convinced that this was only a temporary set-back, and that he would return, Phoenix like, to dominate the English political scene.

The cloak-and-dagger departure of Bolingbroke for France on March 27, 1715, is a far cry from the behavior one would expect from a noble lord of the realm. In great secrecy he borrowed money against his personal estates which were entrusted to six political friends for his wife's use; personal effects such as household items were passed to his wife. Then on March 26, he appeared in full regalia at a London playhouse and was his eloquent best. The following morning, accompanied by a French courier, Lavigne, and heavily disguised as a servant of one of the French ministers, he shuffled into a coach and departed for Dover and his new life in France. There at least he knew he had friends and supporters. No triumphal procession this time from Calais to Paris where the muffled figure was welcomed by Torcy. All efforts to see Lord Stair, the Ambassador, failed as the latter had been warned by London to monitor his activities from a distance. In a long letter addressed to Stair with the request that it be forwarded to the King, Bolingbroke declared his complete innocence of any crime or duplicity, and reaffirmed his zeal and patriotism. On the command of the King he would seek an obscure retreat to recover from the series of misfortunes which had overwhelmed him. His conduct would be without reproach (which was tantamount to saying he would avoid any involvement with the Jacobites or their sympathizers)[14]. An unsupported statement by one of his biographers indicates that at this very time he was having several interviews with the Maréchal de Berwick, the Jacobite representative in Paris, who noted his goodwill towards the Jacobite cause. This, paradoxical as it may appear, was highly likely in view of his later actions. Bolingbroke apparently shared a house in Paris with his friend James Butler, Duke of Ormonde, but soon retired to St.-Clair-Sur-Rhône in Dauphiné where he could well have passed some time with the Abbé de Tencin, and Antoine de Ferriol (Pont-de-Veyle), the son of his great friend. Thereafter he moved to Bellevue, near Lyons, writing to his friend George Clarke that he had moved from Paris to avoid embarrassing his friends. Not appearing to have any fixed plan of action, he was simply waiting for the report of the Commons' Secret Committee which was deliberating the fate of Oxford and himself[15].

Meantime in England, the Hanoverians were becoming very unpopular, and uprisings occurred in several counties. Bolingbroke's Tory friends, Wyndham, Lansdowne and Ormonde, kept him supplied with reports, but they too were involved in Jacobite intrigues and exaggerated or miscalculated the seriousness of the situation. They all believed that the Tory party represented the majority of the country gentlemen, the heart of the nation, and being held in contempt at the royal court, had recourse only to the Jacobite cause. When, in addition, he was informed in June that a motion of impeachment had been unanimously carried, and in August that an act of attainder had been passed (unless he should surrender by September 10), he decided to throw in his lot with the Pretender. In July of 1715 he accepted an earldom from James whom he had met at Commercy and became his Secretary of State. This second gross blunder was to color his future and cause him constant regrets and tortures. For the moment however, he believed he had taken the right step, especially when, in September, after the time limit for his surrender had expired, his name was removed from the roll of peers, a heavy blow indeed. Bolingbroke's tenure of the Secretaryship lasted but eight months and was full of frustrations. Though he was a most diligent and tireless functionary, he secretly detested the Jacobites he met, fulminating against their petty jealousies, their inefficiency and their unjustified criticisms. The Jacobite affair of 1715-16 was a total disaster, marred by mutual incomprehension and blame on all sides[16]. However guilty Bolingbroke was of double-dealing during this adventure, keeping as it were a foot in two camps[17], he never betrayed the constitution or the religion of his own country, heartily loathing the Jacobite creed and secretly desirous of converting his temporary allies to the British system of government and to Protestantism. The death of Louis XIV in August of 1715 sounded, in effect, the death knell of the Jacobite movement, for the Regent, the Duc d'Orléans, who aspired to the throne of France, had no wish to antagonize England by openly sympathizing with the Jacobite cause. Bolingbroke was powerless to change the Regent's mind even though he did his best to win the support of two of his ministers, the Duc de Noailles and the Maréchal d'Huxelles, whom he knew personally. In March of 1716, when Bolingbroke received his marching orders from the Pretender, he was thoroughly disillusioned with the whole business and glad to be clear of it. On direct orders from Stanhope, the English Secretary of State, Lord Stair now fostered this change of heart in order to profit from Bolingbroke's knowledge of the whole affair and to further discredit the Jacobite cause. Bolingbroke who would do anything and betray anybody to further his political ambitions, was caught in the middle of a situation which for him had no happy solution. Vilified by many Englishmen for having betrayed England, he was equally calumniated by the Jacobites he had tried to serve; their reports and accusations were widely disseminated in England. Anxious now only to win the King's pardon, Bolingbroke left no stone unturned to prove himself useful to the British government by imparting his knowledge of foreign policy to Stair and also to Stanhope when he visited Paris. When the Duc de Bourbon assumed power in 1723, he cultivated his friendship in order to further the interests of the Crown and the prospects of his own pardon which he was not to win until 1723.

In this fateful year of 1716 when all must have seemed lost, Bolingbroke wrote his <u>Reflections upon Exile</u> in imitation of Seneca's <u>De Consolatio ad Helviam</u>, where he accepts his fate with philosophical stoicism commenting on the transience of human life, the immutability of the laws of nature, the limits of human reason and the value of experience and example in the solution of life's problems. These are themes that recur in one form or another in all his future works. It was in a small house at Ablon, lent him by Mme de Ferriol, that he was able to meditate and write far from the madding crowds. Towards the end of this year, he frequented the social and intellectual circles of Paris, introduced most likely by such friends as the Duke of Berwick, the Torcys, Mme de Ferriol and the Maréchal d'Huxelles (her lifelong partner). His relations with Mme de Ferriol's sister, Mme de Tencin, were certainly warm and friendly though rather shrouded in mystery. Did he, in fact, become her lover for a short time as Lord Stair reported and as a popular French song of the time would have us believe[18]? Both were passionate natures with disreputable pasts, highly intelligent with an intense curiosity about life but unstable emotionally. This is very likely and supported by his comments in a letter written to Mme de Ferriol somewhat earlier[19]. Scholars he met at this period included Lévesque de Pouilly and Pierre Joseph Alary with whom he had a very warm and fruitful relationship. He may well have met the greatest of them all, Voltaire, but there is no clear evidence to support this. In view of the fact that Voltaire visited him at La Source and became his great admirer, this seems probable. Fontenelle and Marivaux he may also have met in the salon of the Marquise de Lambert, where wits and scholars held forth on their favorite topics in an atmosphere of politeness and good breeding. Fontenelle, the grand old man of Parisian society, the man who boasted that he had never laughed in his life, found little favor with the ebullient Bolingbroke who considered his philosophical system superficial and tawdry[20]. How one would like to have participated in some of these discussions where great minds were coming to grips with the grave problems of the day! It is frustrating that we have so little recorded of the important role that Bolingbroke must have played in the development of the French Enlightenment.

It was in 1716 too that Bolingbroke met his future second wife, Marie-Claire de Marcilly, Marquise de Villette, who was connected by marriage to the famed Mme de Maintenon. A widow for nine years, she had three daughters - the Abbess of Sens, Mme de Volar, and the Marquise de Montmorin. These ladies were adopted by Bolingbroke and became very firm friends with their stepfather. The circumstances of the first meeting are not known but they may have become acquainted through the offices of mutual friends at the Paris residence of the Marquise in the rue St. Dominique. Despite the fact that his first wife still lived, though in ill-health in England, he moved with the Marquise to Marcilly, near Nogent-sur-Seine in January of 1717, though they continued to make frequent visits back to Paris, this time at her new home in the rue du Gros Chenet. She was a vivacious and highly intelligent woman who managed to keep Bolingbroke closely attached to her, if not always faithful, for the remainder of her life. The circumstances surrounding the marriage are somewhat mysterious because the Marquise had financial interests in England, and as the wife of an attainted traitor, her holdings would pass automatically to the Crown. They may have become married as early as

December 1718[21], though Alary denies it. Early biographers report a marriage at Aix-la-Chapelle in May of 1720, but more recent writers seem to agree that a private marriage ceremony took place in the chapel of Lord Stair at Montfermeil early in 1719, a few months after the death of his wife in England, followed by a public announcement only in July of 1722[22].

Acquaintances and friends made at this period include the Abbé Conti, the Abbé Asselin, the Abbé de Vertot, the British mathematician and philosopher, Brook Taylor, the Duc de Villars-Brancas (a future neighbor at La Source), Mlle Aïssé (the main attraction of Mme de Ferriol's salon, often referred to as 'la chère Circassienne' or 'ma gouvernante')[23], as well as several relatives of Mme de Ferriol such as the Marquis de Matignon, the Marquis de Belleroy, the Duc de Coigny, the Comte de Caylus and the Duc de Noirmoutier. Of these, the Marquis de Matignon and his family seemed to have found a special place in Bolingbroke's affections[24]. During this four year period of intense intellectual activity lightened by frequent visits to the social milieux of Paris, Bolingbroke pursued his interest in philosophy and particularly in historical studies, stimulated by his erudite friend Alary, one of Louis XV's tutors by virtue of his friendship with Cardinal de Fleury. In letters to Mme de Ferriol he praises Alary for his great learning, his exquisite manners, and his admirable human qualities[25]. A warm correspondence between the two lasted for approximately ten years when a cooling-off occurred. Alary had been working on Bolingbroke's behalf to obtain a pardon for him from Walpole, but appeared to overstep the bounds when he dared to give his headstrong friend some political advice. Living at Marcilly in a narrower circle but thinking in a larger as he puts it, he alternated between his private studies of ancient history and the social delights of his circle of friends, his 'académie,' who visted the couple occasionally. When Alary paid him a visit bringing books and answering queries on such absorbing questions as the basis of the existing system of chronology and the evidence for ancient historical events, he was at his happiest[26]. During his frequent visits to Paris, Bolingbroke also undertook the education of a fifteen year old kinsman, with the assistance of M. Delisle, the King's geographer, Alary, and masters of the French Academy. Like that of Chesterfield, his order of priorities was firstly, instruction in virtue and honor, secondly, the acquisition of a sound fund of knowledge, and thirdly, training in manners and good breeding.

La Source

In December of 1720, Bolingbroke and the Marquise leased a charming château, near Orléans, which went by the name of La Source on account of a beautiful clear spring nearby, and this was to be their country retreat until Bolingbroke's return to England in 1725. We have a description of the property written by Sheila Radice in 1939 after a personal visit, and Kenneth Woodbridge in 1976, complete with plans of the gardens and castle and subsequent alterations[27]. It was a sumptuous palace resembling the château at Malmaison with terraced gardens, pools, orchards, vineyards, and a wood where Bolingbroke could pursue his favorite occupation - hunting. Mottos and inscriptions supplied by Swift and Pope could be found in different parts of the property. Bolingbroke mentions two which adorned his greenhouse and an alley leading to his apartment[28]. Two of his most distinguished guests have recorded their impressions of host and castle. Voltaire, who occupied the upstairs bedroom during his visits, praised Bolingbroke's mastery of the French language and his easy melding of English erudition and French politeness, while Rapin de Thoyras enthused rather about the delightful atmosphere of the property[29]. When he wished to escape from formal visits and dinners, Bolingbroke could retire to his private ermitage, a delightful retreat situated between the castle and a smaller house which he called the 'maison bourgeoise'. Leased to the Bolingbrokes by the Bégon family (of begonia fame), the estate was bought in 1958 by the city of Orléans and turned into a permanent exhibition of French horticulture under the name of Parc Floral, Orléans-La-Source. Opened in 1964, it contained collections of exotic birds and animals, an exhibition hall, a restaurant, a golf course, and a miniature railway. It is a popular holiday resort for people in the area and from Paris itself. Woodbridge tells us that the house is now a centre for administration, overlooking a French model public garden[30].

Frustrated in his attempt to find any scientific basis for the study of ancient history, Bolingbroke was gradually concluding that it was a futile study for scholars who sought a high degree of probability,

14

if not certitude in the recording of long distant
events. His active mind turned rather to the study of
modern history and to more abstract philosophical
questions such as - What is truth? How can we delimit
the field of human knowledge? What is man's
relationship to the divinity? How far can we trust
our power of reason? Why is evil present in the world
and how can we define the concepts of good and evil? -
all questions which have tortured the minds of the
greatest intellects from time immemorial. In this
relatively unknown field Bolingbroke turned for advice
to Lévesque de Pouilly, though Alary, Brook Taylor,
Rémond de Montmort, the Comte de Caylus (a learned
friend of the Ferriols) and Conti were involved in
these discussions which took place both at La Source
and also at Ablon, the little house of Mme de Ferriol
in Paris. It would appear that Voltaire also
participated in these meetings since he too was a
great admirer of Pouilly, acknowledging his primacy in
understanding and propagating in France the tenets of
Newton's philosophy. Not that Pouilly was a convinced
Newtonian like Taylor. An eclectic scholar, he still
followed the a priori or deductive reasoning of
Descartes in order to discover the truth from
hypotheses and innate ideas, a method which he
recommended Bolingbroke to follow if he was determined
to systematize his stray thoughts and reflections.
Almost nothing has been recorded of these meetings of
the minds - just a reference in a letter to Pope where
Bolingbroke mentions the excellent judgment of Pouilly
and the soaring imagination of Voltaire whose play
Mariamne he had just read[31]. The scenario would have
been fascinating - Voltaire, young and intensely
curious about life, sitting at the feet of the amiable
and learned Pouilly and fascinated by the brilliant
rhetoric of Bolingbroke. Not only history and
philosophy but modern politics and the problems of
everyday existence must have elicited different and
fruitful commentaries from all present. Bolingbroke
would surely have explained the reasons for his exile
and his own political credo, hammering the claims of a
democratic and limited government as the best means
for attaining happiness in this life. And then he
would have rushed off to ingratiate himself further
with Lord Stair and his replacement, Horatio Walpole,
and with the Regent himself in order to further his
chances of a full restitution, for Bolingbroke was
first and foremost a politician and a diplomat, never
relinquishing his ambition to occupy once again a high
government post, if not the highest. Though we do not
have specific dates or references, it seems that

Pouilly, Voltaire and Bolingbroke continued these discussions after the latter's return from a quick business visit to England when his pardon (but not full restitution) was granted in 1723.

The word triumvirate springs readily to mind when we consider the life and works of Bolingbroke. Pouilly, Pope and Bolingbroke were the only three men capable of directing policy on the national level according to Bolingbroke himself who could never be convicted of intellectual humility, while Pouilly, Voltaire and Bolingbroke formed the intimate intellectual group noted above. Bolingbroke was Pope's idol, and many were the discussions they had on political and intellectual topics either at Twickenham or at Dawley which was Bolingbroke's residence after his return to England in 1725 and where Pope was a constant visitor[32]. Bolingbroke seemed to stand at the centre of an international movement of ideas, being indebted himself to Pouilly while at the same time repaying this debt by imparting his own influential ideas and reporting his French involvement to both his English friends -- Swift and Pope. To air his views on the great scientific and philosophical issues of the day, Pouilly was, in 1718, directing and writing for a very influential publication, l'Europe savante, ably assisted by his brother Lévesque de Burigny and Thémiseul de Saint-Hyacinthe. This journal was very much concerned with propagating the ideas of Newton in France which triggered the great controversy between Cartesianism and Newtonianism. A learned man like his brother, Burigny was responsible for many erudite historical works and biographies (Grotius, Erasmus and Bossuet among them). Bolingbroke knew him well, corresponded with him (1723 and 1737), and must have derived great benefit from their mutual discussions. Another brother, Lévesque de Champeaux, was also a mutual acquaintance. Being a great friend of Montesquieu and d'Argenson, he and Bolingbroke would have delighted in profound analyses of the political issues of the day in both countries. From the correspondence between Caylus and Conti we can imagine that there were many lively and heated debates on all kinds of scientific and philosophical questions. Conti, himself a great anglophile (he had visited England in 1715) and a convinced Newtonian, may well have taken part, together with Brook Taylor who was at La Source for part of 1720, in certain physical experiments which Bolingbroke loved to carry out[33]. The triumvirate concept can again be noted, this time with Conti, Taylor and Newton. Taylor who thoroughly understood Newton explained his theories in detail to Conti who, by his eloquence, gave the dry substance fire. Other contacts made at this time were Boulainvilliers, an old friend of Lady Bolingbroke and the main popularizer of Spinozan thought in France, the Chancelier d'Aguesseau, a Cartesian who was the recipient of many works on law and philosophy from Bolingbroke, David Durand, a French Protestant pastor, friend of Pierre Bayle and a visitor to La Source who continued the great work of Rapin de Thoyras after the latter's death, the Rémond brothers -- Rémond de Montmort, Rémond de Saint-Mard and Rémond le Grec, a convinced hedonist whose sensualistic philosophy had obvious attractions for Bolingbroke -- and the Marquis de Lassay, a friend of the Marquis de Matignon and like Bolingbroke an enlightened Epicurean.

The early years of the eighteenth century witnessed the beginnings of what is known as francophilia, a movement which had two distinct aspects. Firstly, there was a craze in England for the superficial side of French civilization, particularly French cooking and French fashions and morals, and young English men of fashion would bring back from their Grand Tour misguided impressions of the French people as a whole (this aspect is often referred to as francomania). Secondly, the more serious travellers, although like Bolingbroke they did not scorn light or heavy involvement in the pleasurable activities Paris had to offer, were conscious of their role as ambassadors who could help to promote in their compatriots an intelligent interest in the literature and culture of a great country. Their francophilia was of course restricted to the intellectual achievements and the social graces of their contacts, since the French were hereditary enemies of the British and their politics quite distasteful. An earlier movement of anglophilia had been noticeable in the latter half of the seventeenth century when the Edict of Nantes had sent French Huguenot refugees into Holland and Britain from which they sent their friends glowing accounts of the superior British constitution and way of life as well as some appreciation of English literature. Religious and civil freedom were to be the passionate topics of discussion in France right up to the Revolution. Admittedly the full impact of this anglophilic movement was not to occur until a few years later, between Chesterfield's journey of 1720 and Walpole's first visit of 1739, with the publication of Muralt's

Lettres sur les Anglais et les Français (1724-28) and
Voltaire's Letters Concerning the English Nation
published in England in 1733 and republished in France
as the Lettres philosophiques in 1734. Many of
Bolingbroke's friends in France were anglophiles,
among them Voltaire, Pouilly, Conti and the Comte and
the Comtesse de Caylus.

The Abbé Conti, though Italian by birth, spent
most of his life in France and was a true cosmopolitan
spirit. In England in 1715, he became personally
acquainted with Newton though relations seemed to sour
when he involved the great man in a public dispute
with Leibniz, and when he dared to publish a copy of
Newton's Chronology in France complete with his own
observations. His justification appeared in the
Lettre au sujet de la réponse aux observations sur la
chronologie de M. Newton in which he invoked the
Bolingbrokes as witnesses of his enthusiasm for the
new theories. His Dialogue sur la nature de l'amour
addressed to Mme de V. (possibly Lady Bolingbroke) is
an interesting defense of Newtonianism against the
rigor of Cartesian philosophy. Feelings, declared
Conti, are merely perceptions and love just an
infinite number of perceptions received by the mind
from all sources. English literature, especially
poetry, greatly appealed to Conti; he translated
portions of Milton and Pope into Italian and was
responsible for several other French translations of
English poetry. Briggs tells us that Pérelle was
encouraged by him to translate the first part of
Pope's preface to his translation of Homer[34], while
the Comtesse de Caylus, when a guest at La Source in
1721, translated into French prose Conti's verse
translation of the Rape of the Lock. How far
Bolingbroke inspired a love of English poetry in his
French circle of friends is a question that cannot
accurately be answered, though it was well known that
Milton and Pope were his favorite poets. Hammond has
convincingly demonstrated the undoubted influence that
Bolingbroke had on Pope's Essay on Man[35], a French
version of which was, a few years later, avidly
devoured by a wide French reading public. Though the
Comte and Comtesse de Caylus did not understand
English, they were cultured people interested in
French and English literature. Letters between Caylus
and Conti tell us that the Count (who was a relative
of Bolingbroke by marriage) had begun to learn English
by 1730, since he wanted to study articles in books
which were untranslatable because of the vivacious and
imaginative quality of the English mind and its

predilection for detached ideas[36]. Pouilly was of course a <u>savant</u> whose wide-ranging interests in philosophy made a study of English authors such as Locke imperative. Bolingbroke took Pouilly back to England with him in 1725, and it is likely that he was a guest at Dawley. No records subsist of his activities during his eighteen month stay, but it is highly probable that he formed a willing part of the intellectual coterie at Uxbridge where Pope was a constant visitor. Another of Pope's idols was the distinguished Lady Mary Wortley Montagu who had most likely met Conti during his 1715 visit and continued to correspond with him while en route through Paris to Constantinople in 1716 where her husband occupied the post of British ambassador. A woman of the world with a large fund of classical learning, a scintillating conversationalist and a poetess in her own right, she would no doubt have played her part in the popularisation of English literature on the Continent. It seems reasonable to assume that she frequented Bolingbroke's circle of friends, though in later life, after a falling out with both Pope and Bolingbroke, she declared that she had met the latter only once and bitterly criticized him as a politician, a writer and a man[37].

Voltaire

The personal relations between Bolingbroke and Voltaire, who at this period was garnering impressions and ideas from a vast library and an extensive circle of acquaintances, have been documented by numerous writers many of whom disagree about important facts. This is understandable, since one of the traits of the French writer was to constantly adopt subterfuges and <u>noms de plume</u> in a mischievous attempt to throw the reader off the track. Expediency may well have dictated this line of conduct as a result of his unfortunate experiences in France, especially in the affair of the Chevalier de Rohan which landed him in the Bastille and was the direct cause of his exile to England in 1726. It is likely that they met at the house of a mutual friend, Mme de Ferriol, who was the mother of Voltaire's school-mate, the Comte d'Argental. We have a letter which Bolingbroke addressed to Mme de Ferriol in 1719, asking her for a copy of Voltaire's new tragedy, <u>Oedipe,</u> about which he had heard so much. He was impressed with Voltaire's boldness in challenging the great Corneille and considered him already a famous writer.

Celui qui débute, en chaussant le cothurne, par jouter contre un tel original que M. Corneille, fait une entreprise fort hardie, et peut-être plus sensée qu'on ne pense communément. Je ne doute pas qu'on n'ait appliqué à M. Arouet ce que M. Corneille met dans la bouche du Cid. En effet son mérite n'a pas attendu le nombre des années, et son coup d'essai passe pour un coup de maître.[38]

It is not certain whether Voltaire and Bolingbroke had met before the Frenchman's visit to La Source at the end of 1722, though the tone of his letter to Thieriot would support an earlier meeting. According to a letter he wrote to Madeleine du Moutier, Marquise de Bernières, and to Thieriot in June of that year, he had intended to dine with Bolingbroke and M. de Maisons at the Bernière's new residence, a visit which did not eventuate[39]. In December he did arrive at La Source after a visit to Le Bruel where his friend the Duc de la Feuillade resided, and spent two days there[40]. Marais describes this visit and the 'lettre merveilleuse' which Voltaire wrote to Thieriot about his famous host, a letter which rapidly permeated Parisian circles. Voltaire knew that Bolingbroke, who was related to the Calendrini family of Geneva, had ended his Grand Tour in this city, frequenting and befriending many Huguenots both there and in London on his return. Thus he was not loth to read him his poem, La Ligue, which was subsequently printed in Geneva and then in Holland with subsidies from Bolingbroke and other admirers[41]. Voltaire's highly eulogistic portrait of Bolingbroke during this visit is well-known:

J'ai trouvé dans cet illustre Anglais toute l'érudition de son pays et toute la politesse du nôtre. Je n'ai jamais entendu parler notre langue avec plus d'énergie et de justesse. Cet homme qui a été toute sa vie plongé dans les plaisirs, et dans les affaires a trouvé pourtant le moyen de tout apprendre et de tout retenir. Il sait l'histoire des anciens Egyptiens comme celle d'Angleterre. Il possède Virgile comme Milton; il aime la poésie anglaise, la française et l'italienne; mais il les aime différemment, parce qu'il discerne parfaitement leurs différents génies.[42]

Significant words! Bolingbroke is already initiating Voltaire not only into English history and literature and Egyptian history, but into what Dédéyan terms 'cosmopolitisme littéraire'[43]. In the same letter Voltaire declares his great satisfaction at the enthusiastic praise meted out to the poem:

> Dans l'enthousiasme de l'approbation, ils [Bolingbroke et Mme de Villette] le mettraient au-dessus de tous les ouvrages de poésie qui ont paru en France; mais je sais ce que je dois rebattre de ces louanges outrés...

Though Voltaire appears to doubt the sincerity of such fulsome praise, Bolingbroke shows that there was no reason to do so in a letter sent to Mme d'Argental the same day:

> M. de Voltaire a passé quelques jours ici. J'ai été charmé et de lui et de son ouvrage. Je me suis attendu à trouver beaucoup d'imagination dans l'un et dans l'autre, mais je ne me suis pas attendu à trouver l'auteur si sage, ni le poème si bien conduit[44].

A.-M. Rousseau has rightly declared these lines perspicacious and prophetic, as Bolingbroke has here defined three fundamental aspects of Voltaire as he appeared to English eyes -- great talent, a lively imagination, but indiscreet behavior[45]. It is interesting to note that Bolingbroke's main intellectual activities at this period were history, under the direction of Alary with a projected history of Europe from the sixteenth century to 1713 in 1724, philosophy, under the tutorship of Pouilly, and religious criticism particularly of the Bible, a threefold program which Voltaire was to carry out himself in the following twenty years.

A letter sent to the Marquise de Bernières c. 15 May 1723, probably from the little house at Ablon, indicates that Voltaire was quite overwhelmed by the eloquence of Bolingbroke who made him forget his surroundings and even his own writings and projects:

> Je crois déjà être ici à cent lieues de Paris. Milord Bolingbroke me fait oublier et Henri quatre et Marianne, et comédiens, et libraires ----.[46]

We can well imagine the content of the long discussions that would have taken place at Ablon between Voltaire, Bolingbroke, Pouilly and others, but it is impossible to pin-point any specific ideas that Voltaire gleaned from his friends and incorporated into his later works. What is clear, is that his appreciation of English literature, history and politics was sharpened to such an extent that he became an anglophile well before his visit in 1726. Baldensperger has finely marked the reasons for the mutual attraction between the arrogant English aristocrat and the proud ambitious bourgeois Voltaire, while at the same time noting the fundamental differences between their philosophies[47]. Praise from an international political figure was meat and drink to the man who was so susceptible to flattery. To demark however the thin line between sincere praise and gross flattery is no easy task. At least Voltaire appeared sensibly moved on Bolingbroke's departure for England in June of 1723 to attempt to retrieve his shattered political fortunes:

> M. de Richelieu partit pour Forges et milord Bolingbroke pour l'Angleterre, ainsi je ne sais plus que devenir dans Paris...[48]

> Une chose qui m'intéresse davantage est le rappel de milord Bolingbroke en Angleterre. Il sera aujourd'hui à Paris et j'aurai la douleur de lui dire adieu, peut-être pour toujours.[49]

This was not to be, as Bolingbroke returned in September of 1723; the two men met up again at Ablon the following year (1724), and Bolingboke returned to Dawley only in 1725.

Meantime, in November of 1723, Voltaire suffered a very serious attack of smallpox, and there is no reason to doubt the real concern of his friend. However, the new method of vaccination had already been tried and tested and was successful in the case of Mlle Aïssé, 'la Circassienne', and also for Voltaire who rapidly recovered. His gratitude both to Gervasi, his doctor, and to his friend, despite the exaggerated classical references, seems quite sincere:

> Et toi, cher Bolingbroke, héros qui d'Apollon
>   As reçu plus d'une couronne,
>   Qui réunis en ta personne
>   L'éloquence de Cicéron,
>   L'intrépidité de Caton,
> L'esprit de Mécénas, l'agrément de Pétrone,[50]
> Enfin donc je respire, et respire pour toi;
> Je pourrai désormais te parler et t'entendre.[51]

The close and cordial relationship between the two men at this stage is quite evident in the long letter (the only one remaining) Bolingbroke wrote to Voltaire in June of 1724 where his attitude appears frankly paternalistic. He counselled Voltaire to read Locke, to be intellectually modest, unlike Descartes and Malebranche whose arrogance vitiated their physical and metaphysical theories (as shown by Huygens and Newton), and to cultivate his great natural talents, stressing once again, as he had in his letter to Pope earlier in the same year, the importance of his powerful imagination:

> Votre imagination est une source intarissable des idées les plus belles et les plus variées. Tout le monde vous l'accorde, servez-vous-en pour inventer. Mais retenez-la quand il s'agit de corriger vos ouvrages ou de régler votre conduite. Ne souffrez pas qu'elle entre dans le département du jugement --- La Nature vous a donné un grand fonds de bien. Dépêchez-vous à le faire valoir.[52]

Paternalistic, to be sure, but also a little patronizing for all its benevolent tone. As A.-M. Rousseau has pointed out, this was not a unique example of the attitude of many of the English aristocracy towards struggling writers, though it was often much less thoughtful[53]. Even at this stage Bolingbroke shows an equivocal attitude towards Voltaire, for Burigny who was present at several meetings between Voltaire and Bolingbroke could write:

> -- je me souviens qu'un jour, on parlait chez un seigneur de Pope et de Voltaire; il les connaissait tous deux également; on lui demanda auquel des deux il donnait la préférence; il nous répondit qu'ils étaient les deux plus beaux génies de France et d'Angleterre, mais qu'il y avait bien plus de philosophie dans la tête du poète anglais que chez Voltaire.[54]

Voltaire's reaction to Bolingbroke's letter remains unknown since his only letter of December 1725 does not mention it. A mixed reaction probably -- pleasure at being highly praised but impatience at the reserves expressed, especially about his equivocal conduct which apparently had been noticed in their early contacts and was to be especially blatant in the matter of the Henriade dedication. Voltaire apparently wanted to dedicate the poem to Bolingbroke at the end of 1725. The latter, while praising the work, felt that a more famous patron was needed (perhaps George I) and wondered about the real intentions of the author in a letter addressed to Mme de Ferriol. A little later he was left in no doubt of his ambiguous actions:

> Ce que vous me mandez de Voltaire et de ses projets est dans son caractère et tout à fait probable; ce qu'il me mande y est tout à fait contraire. Je lui répondrai dans quelque temps d'ici, et je lui laisserai toute sa vie la satisfaction de croire qu'il me prend pour dupe avec un peu de verbiage.[55]

Whatever the reasons for this little 'froissement', the relationship continued to be friendly. It was Bolingbroke who introduced Voltaire's work to his friends Swift and Pope. The former had been invited to La Source as early as 1721 where he was to have met Voltaire, a visit which unfortunately did not eventuate. Pope had already read a copy of La Ligue, sent by Caryll (a mutual friend), and apparently had been in correspondence with Voltaire about the work, though no trace of this now exists. The matter of La Mort de Mariamne is somewhat more complex. In a letter about Lévesque de Pouilly and Voltaire sent to Pope in 1724, Bolingbroke praises the work highly, even more than the plays of Racine and Corneille which he has obviously studied closely:

> I am read[ing] in a tragedy which he has just finished and which will be played this Lent. The subject is the death of Meriamne [Mariamne]; you will, I believe, find in it that art which Racine put into the conduct of his pieces, and that delicacy which appears in his diction, with a spirit of poetry which he never had, and which flags often in the best of Corneille's tragedies. But I will say no more of it since he intends to send it you.[56]

It appears likely from a letter Pope sent to Caryll in December of 1725 that Voltaire did in fact send him the work, but it is also evident from the same letter that Bolingbroke himself dispatched a copy, having in mind perhaps the changeable and mistrustful nature of Voltaire's temperament. In a letter to Bolingbroke dated April 9, 1724, after a scholarly commentary on La Ligue, Pope paid homage to Voltaire as a friend and

24

intimate of Bolingbroke who possessed an 'honest principled spirit of true religion', who honored 'authority and national sanctions without prejudice to truth or charity', and who had 'studied controversy less than reason'[57]. It was the first time Voltaire had been eulogized by an English author, and Bolingbroke was certainly responsible for a large measure of Pope's enthusiasm.

In England as an exile in May of 1726, Voltaire's first night was spent at Bolingbroke's London house in Pall Mall which he used henceforth as a mailing address. He came well recommended by his English host and seemed grateful for all the assistance given him to make his stay a pleasant and profitable one. It is obvious from the records that the impoverished author was not only offered financial help and a home (which he refused since his friends were aristocrats!)[58], but also recommended to Royalty (by Lady Bolingbroke) and introduced to many of the leading literary and political figures of the day[59]. He would have been an occasional guest both at Dawley, Bolingbroke's country residence, and Pope's villa at Twickenham which was in close proximity. Brinsden, Bolingbroke's secretary and agent in England when his master was in France, was well known to Voltaire, as also was Bolingbroke's half sister Henrietta Howard who, with her husband, aided in the publication of La Henriade[60]. Gustave Lanson, in his edition of the Lettres philosophiques, stresses the role that Bolingbroke must have played in the formation of Voltaire's views of the country and its history, though it is of course impossible to be more specific. The question of Voltaire's active involvement in English party politics during his exile has never been satisfactorily explained. The rumor that he acted on occasion as a spy for the Whig government of Walpole was first spread by one of Pope's biographers (Owen Ruffhead), repeated by Churton Collins (Voltaire in England), refuted by Lucien Foulet in his Correspondance de Voltaire and finally admitted as a possibility by A.-M. Rousseau (I, 149-51) if the notion of professionalism were dropped. In view of the fact that he dedicated his tragedy of Brutus to Bolingbroke in 1731, a work which warmly defends liberty against the ambitions of a nascent tyrant (in the English context, this was read to mean the Tory leadership against the arbitrary rule of Sir Robert Walpole), this seems unlikely. However, Voltaire was not averse to frequenting Whig circles as well as Tory, since his infinitely curious mind sought to glean information wherever he could find it, regardless of the consequences. In the Spring of 1727, he did reveal, whether consciously or not is uncertain, the identity of the <u>Occasional Writer</u> which was one of Bolingbroke's pseudonyms in his ceaseless journalistic warfare[61]. This rather soured his relations with Bolingbroke and his circle who could no longer refer to him as a <u>gentleman</u>. Though there is no record of future meetings during Bolingbroke's residence in France (1735-43), Voltaire did not cease to admire Bolingbroke the writer, at least until his death and the publication of his works. He was still 'un des plus brillants génies et l'homme le plus éloquent de son siècle' in 1727-28,[62] a writer who, learned in both languages, had taught him, Voltaire, to introduce into his own writing 'cette force et cette énergie qu'inspire la noble liberté de penser' (<u>Discours sur la tragédie</u> - a preface affixed to <u>Brutus</u>),[63] and later in 1752, 'le plus grand maître de sagesse et de moeurs qui ait jamais été'[64]. After Bolingbroke's death in 1751, the publication of his works by Mallet in 1754, and a French translation of the <u>Letter to Sir William Wyndham</u> (<u>Mémoires secrets</u>), Voltaire's attitude changed drastically, and we have many uncomplimentary references both to the content and to the style of his writings. In his <u>Lettre sur Rabelais et sur d'autres auteurs accusés d'avoir mal parlé de la religion chrétienne</u> he condemns Bolingbroke's violence and 'éloquence funeste' adding:

Il est triste qu'un si sublime génie ait voulu couper par la racine un arbre qu'il pouvait rendre très utile en élaguant les branches, et en nettoyant sa mousse[65]

Yet here again Voltaire could be quite ambiguous. The man who, in 1732, had expressed a lifelong attachment to Bolingbroke[66], could, some twenty years later, write in one breath:

La vigne de la vérité est bien cultivée par des d'Alembert, des Diderot, des Bolingbroke, des Hume etc.[67]

and

... Bolingbroke, Shaftesbury auraient éclairé le genre humain s'ils n'avaient pas noyé la vérité dans des livres qui lassent la patience des gens les plus intentionnés.[68]

How to take seriously such divergent views? A little

26

later (1760), Voltaire calls his work abominable and insolent[69], but admits that Bolingbroke, unlike his contemporaries, was a man of worth:

> ... j'aime autant les livres de cette nation [England] que j'aime peu leurs personnes. Ces gens-là n'ont pour la plupart du mérite que pour eux-mêmes. Il y en a bien peu qui ressemblent à Bolingbroke; celui-là valait mieux que ses livres, mais pour les autres Anglais leurs livres valent mieux qu'eux.[70]

Some years later Bolingbroke's 'lifelong friend' took pleasure in bruiting abroad Bolingbroke's earlier profligate behavior when he was Secretary of State:

> Quand mylord Bolingbroke fut fait secrétaire d'état, les filles de Londres qui faisaient alors la bonne compagnie, se disaient l'une à l'autre: 'Betti, Bolingbroke est ministre!' huit mille guinées de rente; tout pour nous!

Unlike Pope, Bolingbroke was a communicative man, diffusing everywhere his virtue and knowledge, an ordinary lamp which consumes and wastes itself for the benefit of every passenger[71]. However, the numerous references to Bolingbroke in the works and correspondence of Voltaire, whether flattering or not, his possession of Bolingbroke's complete works and four other individual items -- the introductory letter to Pope, translations of the letters on patriotism and on history, and the Mémoirs secrets -- bear witness to his continued preoccupation with his former mentor. His ill-temper on occasion may perhaps be due to the fact that as a mature philosopher and writer he was anxious to minimize if not to deny any early intellectual influence on the development of his ideas while still preserving a glowing recollection of the man's dynamic personality[72]. Yet, if one is to judge by the sole remaining letter of Bolingbroke, the influence is clear and Voltaire all but admits it: "les Anglais paraissent faits pour nous apprendre à penser"[73]. And even his well-known ruse of sheltering behind Bolingbroke's name in the promulgation of his radical ideas (eg. Examen important de milord Bolingbroke) is a tacit acknowledgement of his debt.

Though of different backgrounds and ages, Voltaire and Bolingbroke had much in common - a tremendous fund of energy, a zest for learning, a contradictory and ambivalent temperament, a love of reason, critical acumen, a frankly avowed hedonism, a love of agricultural pursuits (Bolingbroke's famous comparison of the terre en friche and the uncultivated mind in his letter to Voltaire of 27 June, 1724 must certainly have appealed to the future patriarch of Ferney), a hatred of ignorance and superstition, an advanced form of liberalism, and an insatiable curiosity about every aspect of life. Even seemingly trivial characteristics they shared in common -- the urge to conceal their identity in their writings, a natural hypocrisy, a prudence in respecting the forms and ceremonies of their respective religions, a strange amalgam of heroism and cowardliness that seemed ingrained in their characters. Both were poets, critics, historians, pamphleteers. There the similarity ends. While not sharing the dilettantism of a Chesterfield or a Walpole, Bolingbroke was not a serious force to be reckoned with in the literary world. Too often his ideas, rarely original and often disconnected, remained in the theoretical realm, while Voltaire, fired with indignation at the very thought of cruelty, persecution and injustice, translated his ideas into action. The affairs Sirven and Calas are proof that he was capable of being a real crusader in his efforts to aid the oppressed and attack tyranny in whatever form and place it appeared (écrasez l'infâme). Bolingbroke was first and foremost a practical politician and diplomat whose overwhelming ambition was to retrieve the power he had so foolishly lost. The stature of Voltaire was much greater.

Club de l'Entresol

The question of Bolingbroke's role in the establishment and the activities of the important French club, or Academy, called the Entresol is a vexed one. This club was formed on the model of the Académie Française and was to be its political counterpart. The Académie Française had greatly interested Bolingbroke, and Voltaire seemed to regret that a plan to found an equivalent institution in England supported by Oxford and Bolingbroke when he was Secretary of State, had come to nothing. Bolingbroke 'qui avait le don de parler sur-le-champ dans le parlement avec autant de pureté que Swift écrivait dans son cabinet, ... aurait été le protecteur et l'ornement de cette Académie'[74]. Nothing more likely then, than that Bolingbroke should evince interest in the formation of an Academy, though of a different kind and even more suited to his ambitions, which was oriented towards practical

28

politics and administration. It was not a new idea. In 1692 a small Academy had been instituted as a pendant to the learned institutions already in existence - Richelieu's Académie, Mazarin's Académie de peinture et de sculpture, Louis XIV and Colbert's Academies of Science and architecture, and the Académie des Inscriptions. This was a group that assembled every Tuesday at the Luxembourg home of the Abbé de Choisy and included such dignitaries as Dangeau, Perrault, president Cousin, and Fontenelle. Petty and irritating conduct soon caused its doors to close, and it was followed by Torcy's Louvre Academy which had an equally short life. The Regency with its thirst for innovation in every domain was responsible for a sudden break with the stifling past, and this led to the formation of the Club de l'Entresol in 1723 (so-called from the apartment occupied by Alary in the basement of the Hôtel of président Hénault, place Vendôme), a brain child of the Abbé whose aim was an assembly of people yearning to shed the light of reason on all contemporary activities, a perfectly free political society. He was aided in this task by the powerful support of Cardinal de Fleury who enlisted his aid in the education of the young Louis XV. Bolingbroke, in a letter of 6 October 1723 adressed to his friend, congratulated him on his recent election to the French Academy and referred to the nascent Entresol as notre petite société, declaring it to be of equal distinction. It seems certain then that Bolingbroke was at the very least the sponsor and promoter of this club. The idea of a club as opposed to a more formal Academy was an importation from England, and when he returned to England in 1725, Bolingbroke united around him at Dawley a group of witty and urbane friends (Pope, Swift, Arbuthnot, Chesterfield among others) interested in the political and judicial discussions which were the order of the day at the Entresol. Our knowledge of this club is based mainly on the Mémoires of the Marquis d'Argenson (later Minister of Foreign Affairs from 1744-47) who became a member in 1725 and truthfully recorded all the activities that went on there. Most of his documents were destroyed by fire, but enough remain to enable us to form an excellent idea of the meetings. The Discours de Réception of M.L. Lanier on his election to the Académie des Sciences, des Lettres et des Arts d'Amiens, deals exclusively with this club, while the writings of E.R. Briggs supply further information on some of its members. Each Saturday members met for three hours (5 p.m. to 8 p.m.) to read and discuss news from foreign sources, to criticize compositions on pre-assigned topics and dissertations or drafts of works that had been prepared. Those of d'Argenson himself and of the Abbé de Saint-Pierre, doyen of the assembly, were especially noteworthy. The atmosphere was convivial and quite English -- open-air meetings that followed indoor discussions, a roaring fire in winter, an attractive rural setting for summer meetings and always refreshments à l'anglaise. D'Argenson called it a 'café d'honnêtes gens'.

Since emphasis was laid on the practical experience of members who occupied high posts in the political and diplomatic worlds and who had travelled widely, one can imagine how sought after Bolingbroke would have been in this society. Yet there is no real evidence of his membership, nor does his name appear in the list. We incline to think that, like Montesquieu, Bolingbroke would have had an ex officio status and been warmly welcomed whenever he came to Paris from La Source. Since it was in 1724 that he wrote (in French) his Reflections concerning Innate Moral Principles, he may well have read parts of it before the assembly. But if he had a great deal to offer from his unrivalled knowledge of European affairs, he also had much to gain from the meetings. The Club was a training ground in some sense for future political scientists such as Montesquieu, d'Argenson, Saint-Pierre, the Chevalier de Ramsay, the Comte de Plélo, and the Gallican councillor, M. Pérelle. These were the days when the struggle between King and 'parlement', between Gallicanism and Ultramontanism was rending the nation. It may well be true, as Fletcher suggests, that Bolingbroke benefited from his discussions with French minds who were used to treating contemporary political issues from a scientific point of view, having due regard for historical and political traditions.[75] Though he never became a great political theorist, his experience here undoubtedly influenced his journalistic writings. Kramnick, stressing the elitist tendencies of the group which clearly identified itself with the Parlements, is convinced that what he calls la thèse nobiliaire, 'with its glorification of a feudal past, its aristocratic and antibourgeois bias, its preoccupation with decentralization, balance and intermediary powers', supplied a frame of reference within which Bolingbroke could better study his own society[76]. The importance of the group is shown by the fact that Horatio Walpole, the new English ambassador who was attempting

to negotiate an alliance in France, came expressly to
the Entresol to sound out the members on the project
before proceeding to convince the government. His two
hour speech was reported and criticized since this was
not the French way of doing things. Indiscretions,
intrigues, petty jealousies further led the society
into disrepute with the government and it was finally
suppressed in 1731. However, it formed a very
significant link between the two cultures and fostered
a critical spirit of enquiry which was to have a
profound effect on the whole basis of French society;
'nous frondions tout notre soûl' was the expressive
way d'Argenson put it. Janet sums up the influence of
the Club thus:

> Ainsi finit l'Académie de l'Entresol, dont le
> souvenir a laissé bien peu de traces, mais qui
> mérite cependant de ne pas être oubliée, car
> elle a été le premier symptôme de l'éveil de
> l'opinion publique et de son intervention dans
> les choses du gouvernement. Elle coïncide à ce
> moment du règne de Louis XV, où la curiosité, la
> critique, l'opinion s'éveillent de toutes parts,
> où un air nouveau annonce la présence d'un monde
> inconnu --- Ce n'est pas encore l'esprit de
> révolte, tel qu'on le voit après 1750 avec
> Rousseau, Diderot, L'Encyclopédie; c'est un
> noble esprit d'examen et de liberté.[77]

He further stresses that the Entresol was a link
between the seventeenth and eighteenth centuries.
Ramsay and Saint-Pierre followed closely on the
footsteps of Fénelon and the little court of the Duc
de Bourgogne, while d'Argenson led on to Voltaire, to
Montesquieu, and to Rousseau. The gap which separates
Bossuet's Politique tirée des propres paroles de
l'Ecriture Sainte from L'Esprit des Lois and Le
Contrat social is thus bridged in no uncertain
fashion. The Club was in fact 'le berceau' of the
Académie des sciences morales et politiques
established in 1795 as a new section of the Institut
National[78]. One likes to think that Bolingbroke's
contribution, at least in the field of political
science where England had much to teach its neighbor,
was a very significant one.

Return from Exile

On Bolingbroke's return from exile in 1725 as a
restored citizen and property owner though not as a
sitting peer in the House of Lords, he seemed to his

friends Pope and Arbuthnot to be a much more mature scholar. His exile in France, with mentors such as Alary and Pouilly, had wrought the miraculous change ('paulo minus ab angelis' according to the rapturous Pope).[79] Being without any effective influence as a politician, he decided to go behind the scenes and become une éminence grise in his desire to overthrow the government of Walpole. To do this, he founded a newspaper, The Craftsman, in December of 1726, a publication which enjoyed the reputation of being the most influential paper of its day. It became in some respects a forum where Walpole could be attacked without fear of reprisal since contributors did not sign their names. In his excellent study, Simon Varey tells us that contributions signed O (Oldcastle) are Bolingbroke's, and that three essays marked A.O., D.O., and O.D., indicate participation by Bolingbroke together with another author. Voltaire is known to have received and read the paper on his return to France in 1728. Bolingbroke's essays dealt with international as well as national problems, particularly that of preserving balance of power in Europe through healthy free trade and the end of rivalry in local administrations and trading companies. Apparently the journal enlisted the services of a French adviser in London whose name has already been mentioned, Rapin de Thoyras, whose expertise on government was well-known to all parties. An analysis of the archives of the French Foreign Ministry, particularly between 1732 and 1735, clearly indicates Bolingbroke's underground and dangerous involvement with France, directly through the French Ambassador, Chavigny, and indirectly through his superior Chauvelin, the Minister of Foreign Affairs, to discredit the government of Walpole[80]. He was even prepared to espouse France's interests during a period of conflict (the Polish succession) and even the Jacobite cause once again if it would serve his own interests. His acceptance of a large bribe from the French government to pay for his schemes placed him in the same class as Walpole, the corruption of whose reign he never ceased to attack. Had Walpole known all the details he could have ruined his standing with the Tory party and ended his political career forthwith. Another 'underworld' figure with whom Bolingbroke renewed his acquaintance at this period was Saint-Hyacinthe, a Protestant refugee who had come to England in 1722 and remained to carry out a secret commission for the French government, that of examining English newspapers, including the Craftsman, to observe the political mood of the English government. It is likely that Bolingbroke, as director of the Craftsman, had dealings with him, and may have influenced the thinking of the man who was to be later elected a member of the Royal Society of London. Fletcher has clearly shown that the efforts of France to encourage hostility to an existing regime by siding secretly with the opposition were continued (for example by de Bussy, in 1745) even after Bolingbroke's death, and that the French learned a great deal from Bolingbroke's Dissertation upon Parties originally published as a series of articles in the Craftsman and later translated by another French representative in England, M. de Silhouette[81]. Discussions at Dawley with current figures both English and French must have been far-reaching; politics, literature, philosophy and religion were the chief topics, providing plenty of food for thought for all participants. The project of amalgamating the Anglican and Gallican Churches, a favorite subject of Bolingbroke, must have been thoroughly aired, especially as one of its instigators, La Curne de Sainte-Palaye, was a guest at Dawley in 1726[82]. The questions of ultramontanism and political absolutism, so close to the hearts of Pouilly and their mutual friend the Chancelier d'Aguesseau (a convinced Cartesian) and discussed at the Entresol meetings, would likely have resurfaced here also.

Last Years in France

Bolingbroke's disappointment with the partial restoration of his rights, the continued failure of his plans to topple the Walpolian regime, his loss of prestige with his own party and the illness of his wife who had returned to France in 1734, led him to exile himself once again in 1735. Despite his protestations to Wyndham that, tired of the world, he was now leaving the political stage forever,[83] we shall see that his subterranean political activities were to continue unabated in his new home, for once having tasted the elixir of power behind the throne, he was unable to relinquish the role he had chosen for himself. Travelling to France in late May with his friend Lord Berkeley, Bolingbroke was met at Chanteloup (a castle near Amboise in Touraine, northern France which the two had rented for two years), by his wife and friends - the Marquis de Matignon and the Duke of Richmond. From this castle which he inhabited until the spring of 1736, he made frequent visits to Paris with his wife, to Chantilly and to Sens where his step-daughter was the Abbess of

a convent. In the autumn of 1735, he composed his
Letters on the Study and Use of History which was
supposed to be the prelude to a planned work on the
history of his own times, never even satisfactorily
begun. Within a year the process of re-orientation
was complete, and Bolingbroke resigned himself to a
lengthy stay in France. Leaving the rather
uncomfortable castle in Touraine to the Duke and
Duchess of Richmond, the Bolingbrokes moved to
Argeville, near Fontainebleau, a country residence
only a little more inhabitable than Chanteloup, which
they were to call home till October of 1743. Always
restless, Bolingbroke made frequent visits to Paris
where he continued his attempts, this time with the
new British ambassador, Lord Waldegrave, to influence
politics in England and to secure his own full
restoration. When his wife visited Sens, he sometimes
accompanied her, to work and dictate in a small
pavilion that had been allotted to him in the garden.
Here, and at Argeville, he wrote many of his
philosophical essays, including his meditation On the
True Use of Retirement and Study. During this period
he paid several visits to England - from July 1738 to
mid-April 1739 when he stayed with Pope at Twickenham
pending the sale of Dawley, in 1742 after the death of
his father, and in 1743-44 when he went over to secure
his inheritance, make arrangements for resettling in
his ancestral home at Battersea, and attempt a
reconciliation between his beloved half-sister
Henrietta and her husband. Whether or not due to his
incessant activities or his earlier profligate
lifestyle, his health had begun to cause concern
during his exile, and he was forced to seek a course
of treatment at Aix-la-Chapelle on several occasions.
On the way back to France from his last trip to
England (in June 1744) with the intention of going to
Aix with his wife who had come to meet him at Calais
from Argeville, he became very ill and they both
returned to England. His illness was diagnosed as
cancer, and he bore a slow, painful, lingering death
with the greatest of fortitude. The end came on
December 12, 1751.

This period of exile was a busy and productive
one. Bolingbroke divided his time between intense
intellectual activity (philosophy, history, politics)
and recreation (gardening, long walks, hunting wild
boars in the forest of Fontainebleau or the forest of
Montargis with horses and hounds sent over specially
from England). His frequent journeys at a period of
history when travelling was by no means a simple

matter were undertaken freely, without complaint, and often in the interests of others. Friends he always had, both French and English in great number, and when he was not busy talking politics and philosophy, he was actively undertaking the education of sons of English friends at their specific request[84]. A succession of English visitors found the warmest of welcomes at the Bolingbroke estate (wherever this might be at the time) no matter how busy the hosts happened to be. Of these, Lord Chesterfield was perhaps the most famous. Always a great admirer of Bolingbroke he was himself, in 1741, to make an extended stay in France and also engage in a plan of education for his son, godson, and others who were making the Grand Tour. Whether or not Bolingbroke was again involved in Jacobite activities is a moot point since his angry denials never meant much. This was the period also when he became quite convinced that England was sinking into a state of hopeless decadence, a view which saved him from shutting himself off from the world, as he often desired, and led to the composition of such works as Letters on the Spirit of Patriotism (1736) and the very influential Idea of a Patriot King (1738). His political activities in France centred round the members of the Entresol, some of whom he met elsewhere. Dupin, the fermier-général who was his neighbor at Chenonceaux during his time at Chanteloup, was active in the political scene and author of some repute (Observations sur un livre intitulé: 'De l'Esprit des loix'), while his wife, a cultured woman of brilliant personality, attracted many notables to her salon in Touraine. Fletcher has interesting comments on the possibility of Bolingbroke's influence on the Abbé de Saint-Pierre and particularly on the Marquis d'Argenson who was to be elevated to the Ministry of Foreign Affairs just before Bolingbroke's final departure for England. The latter's reflections on the English constitution and contemporary English politics, as well as Saint-Pierre's comments and his preoccupation with the question of patriotism may well have been stimulated by discussions with Bolingbroke[85]. The influence of the Craftsman with the articles contributed by Bolingbroke was paramount in France. Voltaire received copies of the paper after his return to France, d'Argenson studied and translated articles, and the brother of Lévesque de Pouilly (Lévesque de Champeaux, Bolingbroke's adviser in France on foreign affairs after 1744), used the journal widely. The question of Bolingbroke's role in the freemasonry movement is an interesting one.

Though he was acquainted with Chesterfield, the Duke of Richmond (who had set up a lodge at Aubigny in 1735 often visited by Bolingbroke), Bertin du Rocheret, Ramsay and Montesquieu, all masons, there is no evidence to suggest he was a member of the order[86]. However, he must have gained much and given much in political and religious discussions with these friends. It can well be stated that, as a result of his residence in France, and through his numerous contacts, Bolingbroke became identified with almost every movement of the public mind in Europe - with political opinion, with polite letters, with the speculations of science, with the progress of free thought, and with historical and metaphysical discussion.

PART II

BOLINGBROKE'S IDEAS

Philosophy

In his early treatise, <u>Reflections upon Exile</u> (1716), Bolingbroke was already attempting to work out a system of philosophy that would help him bear the burden of exile. The work, full of trite sentiments and superficial reasoning, is yet important in evidencing his interest in a field of knowledge which fascinated him throughout his life. Certain themes can be found in all his later essays - a stoical acceptance of misfortune, immersion in studious activities which can never disappoint, the search for happiness that is not beyond our expectations, the use of unprejudiced reason in our search for truth, the value of experience and example as an aid to reason in solving life's problems, the immutability of the laws of nature which is the stable element in the fluctuating tide of human affairs, and an intellectual humility before the established and unchangeable order of things. A little later he published his famous <u>Substance of some letters to M. de Pouilly</u> (1720) and <u>A letter occasioned by one of Archbishop Tillotson's sermons</u> where he engaged in a wider discussion of the relationship between frail humanity and an omnipotent deity. Concentrating in his philosophical studies on religion and morality, he built on the early foundations a structure of natural religion evidenced in his later essays addressed to Alexander Pope. What is important in these early works is the evolution of Bolingbroke's critical faculty - examine everything that men have accepted as truth and reject what is personally unacceptable. His relationship with Pouilly between 1720 and 1724 may well have been responsible for his desire to establish a well formulated system of philosophy with all the various elements in happy proportion. Truth may be fully attainable; one must learn to accept what can be demonstrated as scientific truth and what must be considered as probable truth especially in matters of religion and morality. Once again we can note the paradoxical quality of Bolingbroke's genius. While stressing the importance of intellectual humility, he proudly boasted that he had discovered and rejected a great number of errors and now knew the limits of the attainable![1] His familiarity with the ideas of Locke,

whose Essay on Human Understanding he must have read
earlier, led him to opt for the sensualist aspect of
epistemology and to posit his theory of high
probability[2]. Here he differed from his mentor who
was, despite his sympathy for and knowledge of
Newtonian principles, firmly committed to the
Cartesian approach of deductive a priori reasoning
from hypotheses and innate ideas as a way of
discovering truth. If reason alone could never solve
all man's problems, then the senses had to be involved
and this meant observation and experiment. Fletcher
has shown, in his interesting article on Newtonianism
in France[3], that Bolingbroke's love of clarity, order
and design inspired by Pouilly, was also due to his
fascination with Newtonian physics. His quarrel was
rather with the concept of innate ideas, the false
procedure that misled the French school of thought by
proceeding from possibility to actuality, instead of
the more logical reverse. He could not accept the
unrealistic notions of the plenum, the universal
fluid, and the tourbillons moving constantly as a
result of some blind force of external impulsion.
Though Pouilly had an excellent understanding of
Newtonian physics, he did not think that the
principles of the great mathematician could be equally
well applied to the study of the mind. Bolingbroke
never questioned the genius of Descartes, though he
thought him misguided. The benefit that he derived
from Cartesian philosophy was a love of clear and
distinct ideas and the discovery of principles to be
used as a basis for practical action. The notion of
geometry in its widest sense was an important
contribution not only to French but to world thought,
and was linked in Bolingbroke's mind to both physics
and metaphysics, subjects which had occupied him first
at La Source:

La physique nous [Pouilly et Bolingbroke] occupe
un peu; mais c'est la Physique qui est fondée
sur des observations et sur des expériences, et
qui est cultivée par la géométrie. La
métaphysique même, mon cher abbé [Alary], prend
une partie de notre temps; mais c'est la
Métaphysique qui est fondée sur des idées
claires et déterminées.[4]

Newton's idea of attraction was wholly accepted by
Bolingbroke; he found his explanation of the universe
so ordered, beautiful and perfect that he wished his
own philosophy could be expressed in a like manner,
though fearing that such a standard would be

impossible[5]. On Locke Bolingbroke never tires of bestowing the highest eulogies, and while he vituperates Descartes's disciples (especially Malebranche), he delights in seeking out French philosophers whose ideas were similar in certain respects. A case in point is Gassendi whose works he had obviously read and who, following the empirical path of Bacon, led on naturally to Locke[6]. The gentle art of persuasion which Locke constantly recommends would certainly have appealed to Bolingbroke, and he no doubt, in his conversations with Voltaire and other French friends, did a great deal to familiarize them with the ideas of the English philosopher. Despite his interest in metaphysics, he is constantly at pains to denounce the sort of abstract study in which Plato indulged and in which both Malebranche and Pouilly had become enmeshed. So he evolved from the Cartesian teachings of his mentor to a reasoned philosophy of his own based on Locke and Newton.

The transition from the Ptolemaic or geocentric to the Copernican or heliocentric cosmogony had changed the whole field of religious and moral philosophy. Man was no longer at the centre of a universe where he was all important, but just a pawn or a link in the chain of things (The Great Chain of Being), closer to the animals than to God (Bolingbroke strongly opposed the Cartesian theory of the automatism of animals). Since this was so, there had to be someone much higher who had engineered the paths of the sun and the planets and assigned to man his rightful, if limited, place in the nature of things. And this being was, in the opinion of Bolingbroke, all-powerful and all-perfect, 'the source of all existence, invisible and incomprehensible'[7]. He had set up a series of natural laws, an infallible system to which His creations were expected to conform if they wished to attain the summum bonum in this life. Having achieved this, He then withdrew from His handiwork and allowed man to work out his own salvation. Thus, for Bolingbroke, the deity was an impersonal God who did not interfere in human affairs. Man needed to keep in mind the first principles, to use controlled reason together with a modicum of faith in the regulation of his own life. Faith, because it was presumptuous to think that man would ever comprehend the workings of the deity, nor should he attempt to ascribe human attributes to an infinite Being. This was quite illogical. The Old Testament was an historical document, full of errors because written by fallible scholars, and even the New

Testament was by no means an infallible guide[8]. Man should use his critical faculty in the use of the Bible as a personal guide. True Christianity as it came out of the hands of God, according to Bolingbroke, 'was a most simple and intelligible rule of belief, worship and manners ... as soon as men presumed to add anything of their own to it, the human alloy corrupted the divine mass, and it became an object of vain, intricate and contentious science'[9]. It was by its very nature 'one continued lesson of the strictest morality, of justice, of benevolence, and of universal charity'[10]. Through different interpretations of the Gospel, many independent sects had evolved many of which appeared quite barbarous to a rational mind. Instead of promoting the peace and happiness of mankind, these new interpretations, often overlaid with human accretions of greed and ambition, led to dissension, hatred, persecution, murder and war. Despite the fact that man will never be able to penetrate the divine mystery, he should use his reason to adduce proofs of God's existence from the scientific facts of the natural world which He established. This would at once demolish the arguments of atheism and increase man's delight and wonder at the beauties of the universe:

> The more we proceed in the study of nature, under the conduct of experimental philosophy, the more discoveries we make of the infinite wisdom as well as power of its Author. The structure of the parts, the design and harmony of the whole, will be a matter of perpetual astonishment, and ought to be a motive to the most devout adoration of that supreme and incomprehensible Being, of God, the maker and preserver of the Universe.[11]

Thus Bolingbroke attempted to steer a middle path between out and out atheism and a form of Christianity which blindly accepted the teachings of the prophets and the idea of divine revelation (orthodoxy). He considered himself a free-thinker not in the sense of a _libertin_ or a _libre-penseur_ which implied irreligion, but in that of an _esprit fort_, one who could profess an innocuous rationalism, believing in a supreme Being based on the evidence of natural law. Though accepting a modicum of faith since man's reason was not wholly sufficient to guide his personal conduct, Bolingbroke never really believed in revealed

Christianity since this, despite his claims to Swift, could not stand the test of reason. However, his stance on this issue often appears contradictory and ambiguous. He seems on occasion to accept the doctrine of revelation up to a certain point though it must be proved by reason. Even the Resurrection (but not the Redemption) and certain of the miracles were accepted by Bolingbroke despite the impossibility of applying the same test. Christ was a Messiah sent to enlighten mankind and He performed some of His miracles to give men proof of His mission. But what of the soul, the concept of reward and punishment in an after-life, and the doctrine of the Trinity? Bolingbroke argued that the first two were accretions from Greek and Egyptian sources and the last a later addition to the Christian Gospel. This approach to the problem of religion was in essence a deistic one but possessed a distinctly elitist and utilitarian flavor common to many others of his generation (e.g. Chesterfield). The few men who were able to search after truth without passion or prejudice should with great discretion, so as not to disturb the public peace, impart their findings to the vulgar throng, thereby ensuring that sound religious advice would act as a moral brake for the passions. Religious conformity for Bolingbroke was a matter of political expediency rather than personal conviction. Without it one would be unlikely to advance far in one's profession.

The base of Bolingbroke's religious philosophy can undoubtedly be found in earlier English writers such as Lord Herbert of Cherbury, Toland, Tindal, Wollaston, Collins, and Tillotson, but also in the French school, especially Bayle (critical approach to sacred history, rejection of a personal Jewish God, idea of morality as independent of religion), Lévesque de Pouilly, perhaps Charron (idea of superstition arising from a low or anthropomorphic conception of God), Saint-Evremond (divine omnipotence and human limitations) and La Mothe le Vayer. The Spinozan influence was of course paramount in the history of European free-thought at the beginning of the eighteenth century. In France Bolingbroke had encountered it principally at the home of Boulainvilliers and must have been greatly influenced by many of his ideas (adherence to the natural law of God, unity of all creation, submission to the will of the deity which would aid man to reject evil and achieve personal happiness).

Bolingbroke's moral philosophy was intimately connected with his ideas on religion. He could never accept the idea of Redemption because he did not believe in the concept of original sin. Man was born essentially good and it behoved him to remain that way by a proper controlled use of his reason. In fashioning his philosophy, Bolingbroke was influenced particularly by Locke but never went as far as him in proclaiming that at birth our mind is a tabula rasa. Having rejected (in essence) the divine revelation of the Bible, he had to find a different explanation for the origins of moral principles. The metaphysical speculations of Plato and Aristotle were as repugnant to him as the artificial theology of orthodox Christianity. The former rested on hypotheses and the latter went counter to the principles of reason and natural law. Wild speculation and imagination had been the cause of distortion in the religious realm; the secret was to restrict oneself to knowledge that was founded on experience or near certainty (high probability). In an early work, Reflections Concerning Innate Moral Principles (written, according to the DNB for the Club de l'Entresol), Bolingbroke adumbrates the ideas which remained virtually the same in his later essays. The extension of the civilized world had shown the weakness of the theological argument that morality was an exclusive feature of a Christian society. However, unless man was guided by a belief in the natural law of the Universe (set up by God), he could never achieve a good moral life and thus happiness. But, Bolingbroke argues, morality (which he equates with compassion and the love for others) is not innate and bestowed by God because it is not a trait common to humanity. Thus it must be acquired by training and experience; external impressions would obviously vary for all men, depending on surroundings, influences, and customs. Yet Bolingbroke was also influenced by Cartesianism with its principle of amour-propre, or self-love which was of course an innate moral principle, an instinct which leads man to seek pleasure and avoid pain. He may even have read the cynical maxims of La Rochefoucauld where he would find self-love reviled as the basis of irrational behavior. But through pure self-love, man could acquire morality or compassion by realizing that others' needs were similar to his own. In this sense self-love is equivalent to self-esteem or dignity, and sympathy for others would bestow a moral trait upon this principle. Self-love could lead to the greatest happiness and peace for all mankind if

42

only man's reason was perfectly formed in all cases, an obvious impossibility in this world. Bolingbroke was well aware of the power of his own passions and realized that very often the tug of war between reason and passion led to the dominance of the latter. It is interesting in this respect to recall Pascal's theory that an uneasy balance must exist between the two for dynamic living. If reason dominates constantly, aridity results, if passion, anarchy, if a stable equilibrium, a passive state.

The problem of good and evil Bolingbroke found particularly thorny. Since God was omniscient and omnipotent, He could only have created a perfect world. But the world was anything but perfect, and this was due in Bolingbroke's view to the fact that, after creating the world and giving man free-will, God had withdrawn and left man to his own devices. But he went further in stating that evil was a relative term only useful as the polarity of good. If God was not given moral attributes (and the idea of an anthropomorphic God was totally rejected), then the problem of evil would no longer exist. Bolingbroke was at once optimistic and pessimistic about life. Optimistic, because he believed that God had created a perfect world, and that by the sound use of his reason and common sense man could achieve, if not the summum bonum, at least a fair measure of contentment in this life. Pessimistic, because he doubted man's ability to act consonant with a rational philosophy and seemed at times to have little faith in human progress. This view was in part a result of his own failure to achieve a position of political eminence and to exercise complete control over his own passionate nature, a weakness which led to impetuosity, poor judgment, and often outright stupidity.

Montaigne, with his belief in the power of reason to conquer the weaknesses of human nature and his frank acknowledgment of the limitations of this same reason in enabling man ever to reach the truth, may well have been Bolingbroke's primary inspiration. The French author attempted to define the conditions for happiness (a reasoned state of well-being) as opposed to the state of pleasure (solely sensual and instinctive). His scepticism (Que sais-je?) was a salutary one, leading him to question all accepted truths and to fulminate against abuses and injustices of all sorts. The main thing, he contended, was to organize one's life in accordance with one's own instincts. At first a Stoic, he gradually evolved into an Epicurean of sorts and had a profound influence on all later writers. In a way he led on from Rabelais (also read and admired by Bolingbroke) who believed that man, over-restricted by ecclesiastical authority, should express himself fully according to his nature, assuming that well-bred, well-educated people would naturally be dignified and virtuous (<u>Fais ce que voudras</u>). Bolingbroke criticized Montaigne however for being too sceptical about man's limited ability to penetrate God's natural law, just as he had criticized Locke for being too uncritical about theological arguments concerning the nature of God. La Fontaine, directly in the line of these philosophers, was at once a sceptic and a hedonist, inviting us to know ourselves and others, to practise compassion and charity, and to enjoy, in a reasonable manner, the joys of life while we can. Descartes similarly (<u>Traité des passions</u>), underlining the importance of will-power and reason over passions, was convinced that the latter were good if approved by reason, bad if not. This was the same ideal as that expressed by Corneille in <u>Le Cid</u>. Despite the influence of these writers, asceticism tinged with intolerance had a firm hold over French thought from Pascal through to the great preachers Bossuet and Bourdaloue, and later to Fénelon. Running parallel to this movement was the <u>libertin</u> current, sceptics like La Mothe le Vayer who rejected miracles and condemned superstition, and Gassendi who believed like Locke that the origin of intelligence was in the senses, and man's attempts at explaining the origin of the universe were quite vain due to the limited reach of his power of reason, but who postulated that man could achieve true happiness by following the path of reason and virtue. Many of these same ideas are to be found in Bayle and Fontenelle. According to the latter, reason could solve almost any problem, rid the world of superstition (including orthodox Christianity), and allow man to achieve happiness in this world (<u>Du Bonheur</u>)[12]. In his <u>Entretiens sur la pluralité des Mondes</u> he sided with Copernicus against Ptolemy, and his lucid and entertaining style was extremely influential in disturbing the traditional concept of man and the earth as the centre of the universe. Fénelon's <u>Traité de l'existence de Dieu</u>, 1713, in which he finds the proof of God's existence in the wonders of nature, in the complexity of the human body and mind, and in the ideas stemming from their interaction would certainly have reinforced, if not

44

influenced, Bolingbroke's own views. Of more
immediate significance in shaping Bolingbroke's moral
philosophy was Pouilly whose work, La Théorie des
Sentiments Agréables, où l'on établit les principes de
la Morale, had a resounding influence on his
contemporaries, including Voltaire, and whose
disciple, Saint-Hyacinthe, amplified his views. It
would be quite impossible to ascribe certain of
Bolingbroke's ideas to any one of these writers, but
it seems likely that he was heavily indebted to the
French school of thought for his moral philosophy,
especially in the separation of the notion of
pleasure from that of happiness.

Bolingbroke's role in the spread of Newton's
ideas, the initial thrust of which coincided with the
period of his exile from 1715 to 1725, and of his own
brand of deistic thought must remain a matter of
conjecture. Although his works were not published
till 1754, many individual items such as The Substance
of some Letters to M. de Pouilly (1720) circulated
clandestinely in manuscript in both countries, and
some were translated into French in manuscript long
before they were printed (e.g. the Preface to his
Philosophical Works). His strong convictions allied
with his international stature and persuasive oratory
undoubtedly impressed many on both sides of the
Channel and may well have won over some uncommitted
minds. His own contemporary Pouilly, while initiating
Bolingbroke into abstract reasoning, benefited in his
turn from their mutual and lively discussions, since
it appears that his Théorie des Sentiments Agréables
had its genesis in these and in Bolingbroke's
Reflections Concerning Innate Moral Principles.
Maupertuis in his Essai de philosophie morale (1749)
echoed Bolingbroke's philosophy of a morality based
on universal rather than ecclesiastical principles, as
too did Mme Dupin (Portefeuille) and the Abbé de
Saint-Pierre whose notion of bienfaisance as an
extension of the pleasure-pain syndrome showed the
narrow limits between egoism and altruism. The
concept of intelligent pleasures, which by contrast
with le plaisir began to be known by the name la
volupté in the early eighteenth century (always
associated in the previous century with sinfulness),
was French in origin though it appears in English
thought as well[13]. Chesterfield, who was formed in
the French school, never tired of recommending this
philosophy to his son, godson and others. As for the
distinction between egoism and altruism, the idea that
consideration for one's fellow beings was a means of

adding to one's own personal satisfaction, an idea not new in itself, was beginning to have some weight in both England and France at the turn of the century. Bolingbroke appears to accept the social instinct of man as a necessary element in his pursuit of happiness, and whether under the influence of his friend's spell or not, Pope expressed the same idea in his Essay on Man. It may well have been that Bolingbroke and Saint-Pierre had come independently to the same conclusions, though the possibility of influence cannot be ruled out.

In reading the literature on the intellectual relationship between Voltaire and Bolingbroke and the possible influence of the latter on the former, one is left with the impression that Bolingbroke acted as a catalyst upon Voltaire at a very critical period of his development. If it is simplistic to state that Voltaire, the philosopher-poet, returned from England a poet-philosopher, it is nonetheless true that the English experience was an invaluable one, and that Bolingbroke and his French wife contributed a great deal towards Voltaire's re-orientation. The lack of adequate documentation may well militate against a definitive statement of their interaction, and critics have clouded the issue by taking sides for and against an influence with no solid evidence on which to base their judgment. Norman Torrey appears, though hesitantly, to deny any influence, while Hurn esteems it so significant that he wrote a book about it. Though he adduces many parallels (and differences) between Voltaire's and Bolingbroke's religious and moral philosophy, there is no real evidence that would point to a borrowing in either field. Certain points of similarity and difference can be made however in a general manner. They both abhorred metaphysics as being an unfruitful field of study which relied on hypotheses and mystification, and they rejected Plato and Aristotle as guides for humanity. Empiricists both, they accepted the Divinity from their experience and observation of the universe and rejected atheism as being opposed to reason. Bolingbroke used the notion of design described by Fontenelle and later by Butler in his ontological arguments. The observation of natural phenomena in a state of harmony and co-ordination must presuppose a higher intelligence. To support this he (and Voltaire after him) adopted a line of Cartesian reasoning in which the existence of a divine being is demonstrated by the idea that man has of it, leading to the positing of a fundamental link between human reason and divine nature. However, the fact that God is necessary as a primary cause (cause première) has been admitted by every nation, especially the Greeks, Indians, and Chinese. In his Dictionnaire philosophique Voltaire develops this theory, leaning for support on the theories of Newton. Both Bolingbroke and Voltaire believed in the omnipotence and omniscience of God and the fundamental goodness of mankind. The immortality of the soul must remain an hypothesis; man had to make the most of this world (which was probably the best of all possible worlds) by the controlled use of his reason. Their deism may have been a matter of rational study and meditation as much as the result of their reading of previous philosophers such as Lord Herbert of Cherbury. While Bolingbroke postulated a natural religion, Voltaire affirmed his belief in une loi naturelle. The search for happiness was humanity's most basic need, but man had to be guided by a moral code which alone would achieve it. The trappings and ceremonies of theology were an accretion which had the opposite effect to that of pure Christianity: man's mind became befuddled and confused by contradictory interpretations. Christianity was not the only religion; much could be gained by a comparative study of religion and the intelligent study of 'foreign' civilizations such as those of India and China. Rewards for acts of virtue or vice were not meted out in a hypothetical after-life but here in this world in the form of inner contentment or a tortured conscience. Morality was independent of both metaphysics and religion but dependent on the way a particular society was structured. Man was a social being and his social philosophy should lead to concepts of liberty and democracy. Self-love is ingrained in us all but should be expanded to include love for others and thus lead to a deeper, more fulfilling sentiment. Progress in this world would inevitably occur as a result of constant and increasing use of man's power of reason. The symbolism of the last words in Candide is an excellent summation of their philosophies - Il faut cultiver notre jardin. By performing his regular tasks, using his common sense, cultivating the talents with which he was born, man can achieve a fruitful life in this imperfect world and set an example which others will want to follow.

Orthodox Christianity, especially the Roman Catholic faith, was vigorously attacked by both as being the source of superstition, persecution, intolerance and unhappiness amongst men. It thrived on ignorance, fostered bondage, and militated against social progress. By instilling into the human soul the fear of infernal torture in an after-life, it led man to abdicate his rights and dignity as a human being. Worse, the confessional took away the control of man's soul and delivered it into the hands of priests, many of whom were dominated by arrogance, greed and ignorance. An examination by both of the history of Christianity supported this view entirely. They favored a pure Church, subordinated to the State, and of all the sects in existence the Anglican faith was the closest to man's needs. Neither desired to overthrow Christianity entirely in favor of an independent, utilitarian and rational code of ethics, for fear of disturbing the social structure. They merely urged that man use his judgment and critical faculties to think for himself, to question established truths and to work out his own salvation. This was a far cry from Bossuet's plea - 'Hors de l'église, pas de salut, hors de l'église pas de morale'. Why should man accept a miserable existence on earth (a corollary of the theory of original sin and rampant evil in the world) in order to achieve happiness in a theoretical after-life? It just didn't make sense. Both the Old and New Testaments were full of errors, contradictions and inconsistencies, the Old more than the New since it was written by different prophets. Many stories recounted in the Old were absurd and contradictory to the body of human experience; the most unbelievable was certainly the cosmogony of the Book of Genesis, while the Deluge was a mere legend or fabrication of the imagination. The Books of Moses had very little moral or historical value. The barbaric behavior of the Jews, with their ridiculous ceremonies and ignoble conception of God, was a disgraceful part of what was supposed to be La Sainte Ecriture. Above all, the God portrayed in the Old Testament was a cruel and barbarous deity, delighting in human sacrifice and repentant only of his stupidity in creating Man. As for the New Testament, the contradictory accounts both historical and doctrinal of the Gospels are carefully noted, particularly the absurd and puerile theological doctrines of Saint Paul. But at least Saint Paul never affirmed, as did the Church later, that Jesus was God incarnate. The doctrines of the Redemption and the Incarnation were carefully examined and rejected; the Miracles, including the Resurrection, were all dismissed by Voltaire as inanities, though Bolingbroke was prepared to accept the latter and some of the former as being proof of the Messianic mission of Jesus. Jesus, of course, was not and could not be the Son of God; this was ascribing human characteristics to a Divinity, thereby lowering him to man's level. Jesus was for Voltaire a Socrates from Galilee cum fanatic who aimed to go down in history as an inspired prophet. He could not find in the New Testament what Bolingbroke praised, truths of natural religion which were of inestimable benefit for human conduct, though they needed to be stripped of dogmatic accretions originating in the earliest days. The doctrine of the Trinity made no sense, while the ceremonies of Baptism and the Eucharist were pagan rites. Such criticisms as have been enumerated above are by no means profound or original; an examination of the Holy Scriptures by the critical light of reason would yield no other result.

The incoherences and inconsistencies of Bolingbroke's philosophy, the inability of Voltaire to acknowledge any debt to another writer, and the latter's determination to express his most radical criticisms under the guise of a pseudonym or behind the authority of an international figure, have no doubt muddied the question of intellectual influence forever. Thus, professing to have profoundly studied his English friend's writings, Voltaire presented his Examen important and La Défense in a way that completely confused the Bolingbroke ethic. Simply to develop an argument, he twists Bolingbroke's ideas round and often negates them to express the opposite view which shows him, Voltaire, in a much more favorable light. For example, he affirms Bolingbroke's denial of the existence of Moses (the opposite was true) and represents him as being much more opposed to the inspiration of the New Testament than he was. However, the fact that he had thoroughly examined Bolingbroke's writings is proof of his great interest, and it is possible that many of his ideas were derived from a reading of Bolingbroke that suggested but did not express these. One example will suffice: Bolingbroke frequently attacked Malebranche for sustaining that our knowledge is not dependent on sensory experience, while Voltaire in his Traité de Métaphysique criticizes the same author for believing that perception can never be the result of objects. One could call this a tangential influence which is no less important for being impossible to pinpoint.

Apart from divergences of opinion on the question of Miracles and the Revelation (rejected by Voltaire but partially allowed by Bolingbroke) and on the metaphysical problem of the relativity or non-relativity of knowledge[14], perhaps the most significant difference of opinion was on the question of optimism. Though Bolingbroke had rejected Malebranche's theory of knowledge, he adopted his views on the existence of evil in a world created by God. The general laws by which God operates sometimes do not seem to take any account of the individual who is thus relegated to a minor place in the scheme of creation; suffering therefore is possible and likely. Bolingbroke goes further by declaring that the goodness of God is not as evident as his power and wisdom. However, we must accept that all divine action is just and equitable in itself even though this view might be repugnant to our own ideas of justice. Goodness is an anthropomorphic not a divine concept. This doctrine of optimism, so brilliantly incorporated by Pope in his <u>Essay on Man</u> (<u>Whatever is, is right</u>), had unquestionably a profound effect on Voltaire, forcing him to crystallize his own views on the thorny question. Bolingbroke was convinced of the real existence of evil in the world, arguing that it was not merely a temporary lapse from a state of goodness as Leibniz suggested in his theory that God continues to shape the world as the best of all possible worlds. However, our inability to understand fully the plan of the universe should not lead us to posit evil as being absolutely irremediable, since it must perforce emanate from the will of God. How to reconcile this theory with the doctrine of the free will in which both Bolingbroke and Voltaire firmly believed? Simply by stating that man's free-will was God-given, and as God's creature his own choice for evil was an unknown aspect of the divine law.

Bolingbroke sought to justify God by declaring that the general laws he had set up and which could not be understood, much less judged according to human principles, could sometimes bring suffering as well as happiness to mankind. All in all however, man should accept his world and adjust to it. Voltaire agreed that it was presumptuous for man to claim to discover the divine attributes (thesis of <u>Le philosophe ignorant</u>), but went further in affirming that the Supreme Being was much more benevolent than those who portrayed him as a God of vengeance believed (<u>La Loi naturelle</u>). He differed from Bolingbroke in saying further that the power of God was limited since there were events such as plagues, famines, and natural disasters that He could not prevent. If such scourges existed through His will, he would be an evil, not a benevolent God. Thus Voltaire excuses the Divinity rather than justifying him, sometimes resigning himself to the Universe as it existed, at others rebelling against it. He vehemently opposed the optimism of Bolingbroke, so much so in fact that, as Hurn has very aptly remarked, his outrage could be interpreted perhaps as an acknowledgment of his obligation to his friend in other respects[15]. While admiring the beauty of Pope's poem, he frankly disagreed with the sentiments expressed and wrote his famous parody, <u>Candide</u>, as a protest against Bolingbroke's doctrine of optimism. The great natural scourges of humanity (floods, earthquakes, eruptions) seem quite pointless and encourage the spirit of revolt rather than that of submission, and why have the good suffered throughout the course of history from horrors such as the Inquisition and the evil triumphed, often acquiring great material possessions? Where was this benevolent deity? In his essay <u>Il faut prendre un parti</u>, he labelled as charlatans all those who followed the doctrine of <u>tout est bien</u>. The resignation of Shaftesbury, Bolingbroke and Pope before their different forms of misery caused a feeling of revolt in this grand humanitarian.

Later in life Voltaire seemed to draw somewhat nearer to Bolingbroke's philosophy by affirming that God was just and benevolent but restricted by the eternal laws he had set in motion and the harsh and obstinate material on which he had to operate (<u>De l'Ame</u>). And in his <u>Lettre de Memnius à Cicéron</u> he affirmed that evil was necessary in the world; God was good but not all powerful. Thus Voltaire was by no means a pessimist, even protesting in the article <u>Méchant</u> of his <u>Dictionnaire philosophique</u> that the evil in the world, while real and often horrible, was greatly exaggerated. The difficulty in comparing the ideas of these two authors is due to the fact that both were subject to <u>revirements</u> according to circumstances and their own mercurial personalities, which led them into frequent inconsistencies. But more important, many of the ideas discussed were in the air at this period of intellectual ferment, and both writers were acquainted either personally or through their reading with some of the greatest minds -- Woolston, Collins, Herbert, Bayle, Locke, Newton,

Spinoza, Leibniz, Malebranche -- to name but a few.
Yet, imperfect and inconsistent as it is,
Bolingbroke's philosophy, religious and moral, was
profoundly studied by the man who had been so dazzled
by his brilliance in early years. There is little
doubt that, through all the eulogies and later
vituperations, as well as the often twisted
interpretations of his former idol, Voltaire had been
strongly influenced, more deeply than he imagined, and
in his influence on all future writers there must be
seen a skein of Bolingbrokian thought. To unravel
this would be well-nigh impossible, but the impression
remains that, because Bolingbroke's moral philosophy
and his life were often at variance, his influence was
considerably less than it might have been.

History

    Throughout his life Bolingbroke never wavered in
his attempt to discover the first principles of
philosophy and the fundamental facts of life. His
object was to work out the relationship between God,
the self, and other men, or society. This constant
aim colored his views on history to the study of which
his contribution was much more valuable. Just as he
had subjected his studies of physics, metaphysics,
religion and morality to the critical light of reason,
rejecting both established authority and the deductive
Cartesian method of analysis, so too did he apply the
same test to his historical researches. What he
discovered in ancient history, in biblical history
(which, he insisted, should be treated no
differently), and indeed in history up to the end of
the seventeenth century was the tendency to amass
piles of facts (such as lists of events with dates,
names of princes and ministers), assembled often in a
disorderly fashion in an inartistic and boring
narrative. What he missed were the links between
events and actions, the reasons for them, the ideas
and principles that lay behind them. These, if given,
would light up the whole account and make it
infinitely more meaningful. His was an organic,
dynamic view of history as a dual cyclical process of
revolution and evolution, evolution and revolution,
giving rise to periods of barbarism and civility,
ignorance and knowledge in never- ending sequence.
But historical situations do not exactly recur, and
one must beware of applying too rigidly any
generalizations formed from past experience. This
sense of historical relativism which stemmed from
Bolingbroke's awareness of living in a generalized

historical process saved him from the error of applying arguments that were relevant to past history to the circumstances of his own day.

Such a scientific, or philosophical approach to the study of history was not of course an entirely new idea, though its full expression in a major treatise (Letters on the Study and Use of History) was certainly a departure from tradition. Saint-Evremond, Pouilly, Alary had been responsible in different ways for leading Bolingbroke along this path, while his familiarity with the ideas of men like Fontenelle (Sur l'histoire), Fénelon, and his friend the Comte de Boulainvilliers (Lettre à Mlle Cousinot), showed him that it was the genius of each nation that needed attention, its ideas, opinions, passions and ways of life. Facts of course were necessary, but these could be consulted in dictionaries, encyclopedias and archives and interpreted judiciously by the historical researcher. Both Bayle and the Abbé de Saint-Réal, whose works Bolingbroke had studied, had postulated the importance of the critical approach to historical study, and may well have reinforced, if not influenced, his own thinking. The most successful method, according to Bolingbroke, would be to chart a middle path between two extremes -- absolute credulity and absolute scepticism (or pyrrhonism) -- just as he had, in his philosophical studies, avoided the twin and opposing reefs of blind faith and out and out atheism. Since the study of history should be carried out on a scientific or philosophic basis, it was well-nigh impossible to give any credence to ancient history and chronology where the overlay of myths and fables concealed the real facts. Biblical history with its reliance on oral tradition was a case in point. Furthermore, the early history of Judaism and Christianity must be suspect, since writers in all ages had purposely and systematically falsified it for their own ends; partiality and prejudice had led to a myriad of errors, both voluntary and involuntary. However, keeping to his middle path, Bolingbroke sensibly understood the need to check all historical evidence and make a critical assessment of what was genuine and valuable and what was not. His preference lay in the field of modern history, and he planned but never wrote a detailed history of his own times. It seems that even in this field documentary evidence was very difficult to obtain, and he ended by writing a history of Europe from 1659 to 1713 to which he added his own reflections on the nature of historical study.

Bolingbroke's view of the function of history was not, however, primarily to discover how men had thought or lived in the past. Being an active politician who had thought deeply about the nature of his craft, he looked on it rather as Chesterfield did, as a school for aspiring diplomats and statesmen. But since there were many periods of history which had absolutely no relevance in this connection, much, or even perhaps the greater part of recorded history could be ignored, a second, and more cogent reason for his neglect of ancient history. But there was another peculiar to Bolingbroke. His political misfortunes never ceasing to rankle in his mind, he intended to justify his conduct by concentrating on a modern history, politically oriented, in which he had played a considerable role. There was also a second side to this utilitarian view of historical study, an aspect which stemmed from his philosophical credo. Rather than study history solely for one's own enjoyment or even to combat the spectre of gross ignorance of the past, it was important to learn from the lessons taught in order to inculcate in oneself and others private and public virtue and to lay a foundation for future action. However, the emphasis was still on the preparation for the budding politician. This training would improve the mind, sharpen the judgment and the wits, and develop character by removing such evils as prejudice, superstition and intolerance. Thus a distinction could be made between the causes and results of specific events and actions and a knowledge gained of underlying principles. Then a plan of political action which took due account of moral virtues could be devised and followed. This is the meaning of Bolingbroke's famous phrase -- History is philosophy teaching by examples[16].

The idea of historical pyrrhonism already in embryonic form in The Substance of some Letters and clearly expressed in his Letters belongs, as A.-M. Rousseau has indicated[17], to the intellectual climate of the early eighteenth century. No doubt it had been freely discussed by Voltaire, Bolingbroke and their friends, but the principles had already been laid down by Bayle, Fontenelle, Lenglet-Dufresnoy and Fréret. However, in his plan for a general history of Europe, Bolingbroke aimed to trace the political history of Europe from the sixteenth century as an introduction

54

to a history of the first twenty years of the eighteenth century, applying the same critical methods that would have been used to investigate a more distant past. This vast project was eventually to be executed by Voltaire. Absolute pyrrhonism as professed by Bayle was rejected by Voltaire and Bolingbroke who preferred to use their judgment to assess the worth of any particular testimony and establish the degree of certitude. Bolingbroke's view of history as a study of what Fletcher calls 'burning topicality'[18] stemmed from his discussions with Alary, an expert on chronology and ancient history, Pouilly, and the Abbé de Vertot, while his enthusiasm for modern history was due in part to his reading of modern historians, specially Guicciardini and Machiavelli with whom he felt a strong affinity.

The question of 'degree of doubt' that should be expressed vis à vis of what had always been accepted as 'historical facts' was one that occupied many learned minds of the time. The theory that probability is closer to certainty than possibility is to probability was one that appealed particularly to the French mind (its linguistic aspect can be seen in the use of the indicative for notions of certainty and probability and the subjunctive for possibility). Historical certainty can never be achieved since man's concept of reality comes not absolutely, but only through his senses. One can however establish a high order of probability as opposed to a low degree which borders on the hypothetical. This was Fréret's view and also Pouilly's. It would appear that Bolingbroke stands between the two, influenced or at least supported by the former, and influencing the latter in his discourse on the lack of certainty in dealing with the first five centuries of Roman history, delivered to the <u>Académie des Inscriptions</u> in 1722[19]. Voltaire later, obviously mindful of his historical discussions with Bolingbroke and Pouilly, takes up this point in an article of the <u>Dictionnaire philosophique</u> (<u>Histoire</u>). While sometimes rejecting ancient history completely as being impossible to verify and useless as a guide to the modern statesman, Bolingbroke paradoxically adduces parallels between Roman and Modern English history, praising the sense of manly <u>virtù</u> in the former that is most worthy of emulation. And his avowed intention (in a letter to Alary in 1717) was to treat modern history in the light of conclusions taken from his study of the ancient world. He was supplied with information on the Roman Senate by Vertot, while Alary's profound knowledge of Greek and Roman literature was used to great success in contemporary political issues[20]. The famous quarrel of the ancients and moderns which divided the French social and literary world in the later years of the seventeenth and the early years of the eighteenth century did not go unnoticed by Bolingbroke. Already in 1688, Fontenelle had published his <u>Digression sur les Anciens et les Modernes</u>, and Parisian intellectual society which in the 1720's and 1730's centred round the salon of the Marquise de Lambert in the Hôtel Colbert, took up the cudgels. The main issue seemed to be that of Homer translation with Mme Dacier espousing the cause of the ancients and Houdard de la Motte that of the moderns. Bolingbroke's letter to Mme de Ferriol[21] indicates that, while he sided with the moderns (but only after careful consideration), he did not wholly agree with Motte's finding in his <u>Discours sur Homère</u>. Pope, in his preface to volume I of <u>The Iliad</u>, had already in 1715 acknowledged Bolingbroke's helpful criticisms.

Thus evolved, slowly but surely, Bolingbroke's philosophy of history founded on a scientific and rational basis. The removal, or rather the explanation in terms of natural law of the supernatural elements, had already been advocated by French writers in the seventeenth century; in his <u>Histoire des Oracles</u>, Fontenelle had restricted himself to exposing the absurdities of ancient superstitions, though readers found in his exegesis an implicit criticism of Christianity. In the previous year his <u>Entretiens</u>, with its support of the Copernican theory of the universe, had already created quite a stir in French society. What fascinated him particularly was the working of the human mind throughout history, an interest which both Bolingbroke and Voltaire heartily endorsed. Saint-Evremond, whose tolerant deism and epicurean tastes had earlier struck a responsive chord in Bolingbroke, had been quite explicit in his view that an historian should study and interpret social and intellectual currents rather than compile facts and dates which, however, should have their proper place in a narrative, and he was followed in this view by Fénelon, Fontenelle and Boulainvilliers. Bolingbroke's view of history as philosophy teaching by examples was echoed by Voltaire's assertion that history must be studied <u>en philosophe</u>. In the preface to the French edition of Bolingbroke's letter to <u>Sir William Wyndham</u> (<u>Mémoires secrets de Mylord Bolingbroke</u>, 1754), the editor assigns a predominant place to Bolingbroke in the

promulgation of the idea versus fact theory[22]. On the
other hand, the historian must never go to the
opposite extreme by filling his account with
subjective comments which would be rather the province
of the mémorialiste or the annaliste. The idea of the
links between events and actions, the notions of cause
and effect had already been treated by earlier
historians such as Bossuet, though the deists had
rejected his notion of Divine Providence interfering
in human affairs. The continuum approach which was a
natural extension of the link theory may well be an
influence of Cartesianism which dominated the thought
of writers in the second half of the seventeenth
century - there just had to be an order in the
arrangement of human affairs if one accepted that God
had provided man with a natural law. Thus a haphazard
treatment of history as a series of isolated events
and actions would make very little sense. Le père
Rapin, in his Instructions pour l'histoire (1677), had
seen a dual order in the writing of history: a natural
chronological order (ordre des temps) and, more
important, a rational order in the arrangement of
events (ordre de raison), leading him to posit an
anthropomorphic conception of history (the members of
a body being naturally interconnected). Fénelon, in
his famous Lettre à l'Académie (1716), and Rapin de
Thoyras in his Histoire d'Angleterre (Préface), took
up the same theme of the liaison naturelle which would
lead the historian, and his reader, through the
tangled labyrinth of seemingly isolated facts.

Bolingbroke's view of the didactic or utilitarian
function of history was by no means original, being
quite common in the works of the moralist historians
of the seventeenth century and in those of their
eighteenth century successors. Le père Rapin, Le
Gendre, Fénelon, Boulainvilliers and Voltaire are all
convinced of the ethical value of historical study
which aids men to evaluate virtuous actions and avoid
the disastrous consequences of vice. This could well
be the main lesson one learns from history, the one
eternal value in an ever-changing, though recurring,
cycle of events. By applying scientific principles,
one could reflect on the past, observe the present,
and judge the future, as Bolingbroke was fond of
repeating, a sort of selective process that would
avoid anachronistic weaknesses. This was of course a
political expedient as well as an historical principle
and could lead to peace and happiness for all mankind
(such, for example, was the Utopian view of the Abbé

de Saint-Pierre in his Projet de paix perpétuelle).
Thus it behoved the rational and moral historian to
act as a teacher in his actions and in his writings.
It goes without saying that the sort of history which
would have the most significant moral impact would be
political history. By noting the rise and fall of
different types of governments, man could learn what
to accept and what to reject in order to reach his
full status as a responsible citizen. Here,
Bolingbroke was following in the footsteps of Fénelon
and leading on through Boulainvilliers to Voltaire.
In his article Histoire of the Dictionnaire
philosophique, the latter severely criticizes the
Jesuit historian, le père Daniel, who failed to see
the drastic change in human affairs over the period of
years. Strangely enough, the Observations critiques
sur l'histoire de France attributed to Daniel and an
assistant, may have been written by Mézeray, the
author of a later work (1732) on the history of France
and greatly praised by both Bolingbroke and Voltaire
for his excellent civic record. It is very likely
that Boulainvillier's study, Histoire de l'ancien
gouvernement de la France ... published eight years
before the Letters on the Study and Use of History,
exerted a considerable influence on Bolingbroke, for
we see here, in embryo, the famous notion of
patriotism used in the Bolingbrokian sense. If, in
fact, history was 'la mère de la politique et de la
science du gouvernement', this was an essential study
for the man who aspired to the reins of power. The
essential difference between such histories in France
and England was that the former were aimed at the
absolute sovereign in the hope that he would act in a
civilized manner, while the latter were of benefit to
all members of a free society.

Although Bolingbroke's Remarks on the History of
England (1730-1731) are, in a way, like the French
histories mentioned directed towards an absolute
tyrant (Walpole), he is concerned above all with human
liberty. His mind freely roamed beyond the borders of
England and even European history to embrace a world
view which clearly was quite unusual for his time and
undoubtedly had a powerful impact on his
contemporaries, especially Voltaire. While he did not
subscribe to the view that much of recorded history
could be more or less blotted out as being
unverifiable and therefore alien to man's pressing,
everyday problems (a logical extension of
Bolingbroke's utilitarian and didactic view),
Voltaire's achievement was to write the work that

Bolingbroke never did, and by so doing, to formulate a series of general ideas and construct a scheme of universal history which was to become distinctive of eighteenth century historical thought. If historians were to abandon concepts of custom and sovereignty, of the origins and ultimate authority of law which had previously bound the present to the past, a new conception of history had to be adopted; the generalization theory was one way of preserving a vital link between the ages. Voltaire was not alone in pursuing Bolingbroke's ideas on 'total' history - religious, civil, military, diplomatic, moral; Vico and the Göttingen and Edinburgh professors were doing likewise, while Montesquieu went further still in basing the study of history on economic, physiological and psychological factors. This departure from tradition was to be of the greatest importance for the future, since historians, in generalizing about periods of history, supposed each of them to have been governed by certain general characteristics, and further, that there was a kind of logic about the way one period succeeded another, leading them to seek an explanation of the transformation of one into the other. It was one thing to reconstruct the institutions of a long gone period of time, another to show how they had evolved into something different. As Pocock puts it:

> Eighteenth century historians - Vico, Voltaire, Montesquieu, Millar, Schlözer - were able, each in his way, to observe that, in a period supposedly governed by certain characteristics, it was natural that certain social institutions, certain habits of thought and forms of art should exist in conformity with the dominant characteristics and that they should fall and be replaced by others as the character of the period changed.[23]

All that remained was to show how the actions of men could contribute to altering the pattern of the age. Burke will later criticize Bolingbroke for ignoring the common-law concept of custom and all the painstaking work of earlier legal historians and antiquaries which should have provided lessons in plenty. For the moment Bolingbroke's influence on Voltaire seemed generally accepted, for while the comments of a Bubb Dodington seem excessive[24], it was common knowledge, at least in England, that Bolingbroke was the model on which Voltaire patterned his work. Maty finds an interesting parallel between the two men:

> J'y ai trouvé [in the letters on the Study and Use of History] tout l'accord qu'on devait se promettre de deux grands hommes longtemps amis et accoutumés à envisager certains objets de la même manière. Il y a cependant plus de descriptions dans l'un et de réflexions dans l'autre; celui-ci paraît avoir fait la principale étude des hommes, celui-là, des Etats; le poète raconte les événements qui lui ont été rapportés en historien éclairé et aussi impartial que le peut être un Français; l'Anglais est un philosophe profond, un politique adroit, un orateur véhément qui démêle l'origine, l'enchaînement, les suites des révolutions et qui ne se montre pas moins animé du désir de se justifier que de celui d'instruire.[25]

A.-M. Rousseau sums up the interaction between the two as follows:

> Après réflexion, on s'aperçut que le nom de Bolingbroke était surtout synonyme de critique destructrice d'une histoire fondée sur la _Bible_, et relevait plutôt de la théologie. Finalement, par une série de coïncidences, d'affinités et d'interactions, les idées de Bolingbroke, grâce à Voltaire, ont pu passer dans la pratique et connaître une plus grande fortune que celle à laquelle la chronologie et la discrétion de leur genèse semblaient devoir les destiner.[26]

It seems impossible today to decide whether Bolingbroke actively influenced Voltairian historical thought (even though Voltaire had read and studied the famous _Letters on the Study and Use of History_ and the _Remarques sur l'histoire de l'Angleterre,_ a selection of translated extracts from the _Craftsman_ which had appeared in the _Bibliothèque Britannique_, XXI-XXII, July-December 1743), or whether their approaches to the study of history just happened to be similar. What seems probable, as in the case of Voltaire's philosophical views, is that Bolingbroke acted as a catalyst, awakening Voltaire's interest in history at an early age and discussing with him the ideas of the writers in both France and England who were struggling to discover a new historical process. Ira Wade is probably correct in suggesting that Voltaire echoed many of Bolingbroke's views on history and its utility, the condemnation of excessive erudition, the espousal of modern rather than ancient history, the development of a critical or Pyrrhonic view of ancient so-called historical facts, the insistence upon the moral value of the study, and the desire to foster a history of the sciences and the arts, a history of civilizations[27]. He further points out, following in the footsteps of Brumfitt and Nadel, that Voltaire had a much wider concept of history and was by far the greater historian. Voltaire foresaw the merging of English thought and French art into a European civilization and this into a world civilization which no longer rejected ancient history as being unimportant. In emphasizing the importance of non-European civilizations such as those of India and China, he is in reality bringing about what Brumfitt calls 'the Copernican revolution in historiography', displacing 'the Christian European from his comfortable seat at the centre of the universe'[28]. Neither Bolingbroke nor Voltaire possessed a psychological or imaginative view of history; the distance from them to Michelet and Taine is just as great as that between them and Bossuet. While Bolingbroke's mind remained in the dry area of historical generalizations, Voltaire's leaped forward to a more creative view where thought is projected into being, and being into action, positive action such as the striving for freedom in all of its original manifestations. Both Bolingbroke and Voltaire fall short of establishing a real philosophy of history in the way that Montesquieu did, elaborating a theory of the forces determining human development, or of working out a blueprint of human progress achieved by Turgot and Condorcet. Doubt and affirmation bedevil their attempts to be fully consistent in such matters as the authority of the past, the unchanging nature of man, and the application of eighteenth century standards of morality and propriety to the study of history. Yet, in their belief in the responsibility of each man for his own soul, they mark an important transition from the religious historians of the past to the creative historians of the future.

Politics

It is probably true to say that Bolingbroke was a better historian than he was a philosopher, but a better political pamphleteer than he was an historian.

In all his writings on politics he attempted to apply his philosophic principles while using the historical approach to support his arguments. Most of his work is colored by his own intense, lasting interest in politics, his political ambitions, and his violent antipathy to the Walpolian regime. From his philosophical studies he was led to reflect upon the nature and origins of political science and civil government. For him, the basis of all political theories was or should be the concept of the law of nature which had been laid down by God as a model to be followed by all political societies and their leaders. All human laws should follow this natural law of God to ensure the greatest good of humanity. If this were done (and it meant going back to first principles) then public and private morality would be ensured. The words 'clear', 'reasonable' and 'universal' often occur in Bolingbroke's works in connection with God's natural law and the human laws modelled on it. For Bolingbroke, going back to first principles meant returning to the ideal government of Anglo-Saxon society from which modern governments had badly strayed. The system in force in 1688 was the closest approach to the ideal in many ways, but it had been badly subverted by the corruption of the present regime. Bolingbroke was never under any illusion however that a perfect government could be achieved, human nature being what it was; he was painfully aware of his own deficiencies and imperfections. What he urged however was that each man be vigilant in ensuring that his own life be directed as far as possible by a reasonable virtue, while princes and sovereigns should support public and private morality. Change and decay were of course irreversible; one had to be content with the best of all possible systems.

Pursuing his historical approach to the question of civil government, Bolingbroke was convinced that, far from living in a brutish, anarchic and highly competitive state before the establishment of civil society, early man was fundamentally a social being endowed with reason, albeit in primitive form, with self-esteem, and with instinctive benevolence. Thus he was drawn into family units having a paternalistic head with subordinate members obeying his injunctions, and later into larger social units with a more complex hierarchy developing in proportion to the increasing evolution of his power of reason. Civil government thus slowly developed, an artificial creation in which all members did not have an equal share in decision-making, nor were they all free and equal.

62

Heads of important families arranged a contract among themselves, and this was the basis of social and political life. Early governments, by consulting the needs of their subjects, attempted to follow the law of nature and work for the greatest good of their people. Peace, order, and justice were their primary goals. Bolingbroke is at pains to show that the first rulers had been great philosophers and legislators who subordinated their own desires and ambitions for the benefit of all. His contract theory was in opposition to that of Locke who had maintained that civil government was a matter of common consent in order to preserve individual freedom and equality. These, in Bolingbroke's view, had never existed in natural society and thus could never be part of the original contract. Thus, instead of looking forward to an age of progress where all men would be politically and socially equal, Bolingbroke looked back to the Middle Ages where the contract required the government to consult the good of the people and not to defend individual rights and property. His theory, far from being democratic, was elitist and paternalist. Authority should be in the hands of men of superior reason (like himself), and the masses, whom he always despised as being ignorant, superstitious, dependent on their instincts and lacking in judgment, should submit to their decrees, but only as long as these decrees were in the common interest. If they failed to guarantee liberty, the contract should be broken by the landed gentry who were the natural leaders. Individual freedom, self-interest and competition were not beneficial to civil society; they produced the moneyed men, the newcomers of no pedigree or breeding who were not fit to govern.

While Bolingbroke was convinced that all men were not born free and equal, he passionately defended the notion of political freedom throughout his life. This was fostered particularly by his wide reading and his experiences in countries like France where the people were virtually enslaved. He always considered that freedom should be a right and not a privilege for all people. His own awareness of the vital importance of liberty was enhanced by the knowledge that France, initially one of the freest of countries in its Gothic past, was now decaying under an absolute and tyrannical monarchical system, and that England, if it continued to be ruled by a Walpole, might well be in danger of losing its free heritage. Since the good of the people was, in Bolingbroke's view, the true end of government, and the greatest good of a people was their freedom, it stood to reason that despotism was the complete antithesis of liberty and must be vigorously attacked and destroyed. The masses were often to blame however; their lack of intelligence and common sense only helped to strengthen the bonds of their servitude. The role of the King or the Prince in government occupied a great deal of Bolingbroke's attention. If one accepted the premise that human law should conform to God's law of nature, then the ruler must derive his authority from this source and continually exercise his reason to ensure order, justice, and peace in the realm. The doctrine of divine right was anathema to Bolingbroke; God, having instituted his natural law, simply did not interfere in the ways of man and accord a favored place to any one human being. It had not worked in England and it was not working in France and other countries. A good ruler should be a philosopher or a least have philosophic advisers. If man was constantly guided by reason, the perfect form of government would be a republic or an elective monarchy, but since human nature was fallible, a limited, or hereditary monarchy would best lead to political stability. The sovereign's authority must be limited by the constitution, perhaps in the form of a contract with the people. The Constitution should be a balanced one, resting on the mutual independence of the functions of government. His ideas on a mixed constitution of Crown, Lords and Commons and the balance of powers were often confused, though he frequently advocated the sharing of legislative and executive functions by the three estates. The latter should exist in a delicate balance so that no one unit could usurp the power and privileges of the others. To remain balanced they thus had to remain mutually independent. Bolingbroke was ever fearful that the Crown might try to erode the independence of Parliament as it had often done in the past.

In his <u>Dissertation upon Parties</u> which ranks as one of the best political tracts of the eighteenth century, Bolingbroke argued that party labels whose origin could be traced to the religious and constitutional disputes which had been a divisive force in English politics since the sixteenth century, were no longer valid in present-day England. The Revolution of 1688 had, in his view, seen the end of these differences when both parties had been compelled to unite in the interest of the nation. If there was a division in his own time it was a mythical one of

Walpole's own making; the question at issue was really the conflict between a corrupt ministry and the nation as a whole. Distinctions between Whigs and Tories based on doctrines of divine right, hereditary succession and non-resistance, no longer made sense, since all men accepted the revolutionary concept. Bolingbroke advocated the formation of a national or country party which would be in permanent opposition to the Court as a genuine alternative government which would safeguard the nation's liberties.

It is time therefore that all who desire to be esteemed good men, and to procure the peace, the strength, and the glory of their country, by the only means by which they can be procured effectually, should join their efforts to heal our national divisions, and to change the narrow spirit of party into a diffusive spirit of public benevolence.[29]

He soon recognized that, however laudable in principle, this idea was quite impractical. All a national party could do was act as a watchdog of the constitution, since the Walpole regime with its vast system of patronage and corruption was too firmly ensconced to be immediately ousted. Then too the opposition was seriously divided and the spirit of patriotism appeared to be decaying badly. Yet Bolingbroke was still optimistic at this stage, and once again stressing his belief in the universal law of nature, declared in A Letter on the Spirit of Patriotism that all good men of superior virtue should gird themselves, recognize the seriousness of the situation, and stand together in active opposition to bribery and corruption. He was particularly vituperative of the moneyed men and the placemen who put self before national interest and subtly influenced the ministers to corrupt the one body which should by its very nature be incorruptible, the Parliament.

Bolingbroke's idea of the Patriot King, which he consciously derived from Machiavelli's Prince, was a serious effort to integrate his political aims with his general philosophy on the nature of government. Unlike Machiavelli, he did not believe in a radical rebuilding of a corrupt constitution, just a restoration or a revitalizing of the ancient pure form. By writing such a Utopian work, Bolingbroke seems to have admitted defeat in his attempts to build a viable national party with the imperfect materials at hand. Where would a nation find such a leader, perfectly principled with no bias or prejudice towards any party, ever vigilant of the nation's welfare, physical and spiritual, surrounded by wise ministers who would assist him to maintain the balance of power, encouraging trade and commerce while ensuring that an overabundance of material prosperity would not weaken his people's moral fibre? Once again in this work, Bolingbroke was taking refuge in the past, yearning for a revival of the ancient and pure constitution. What he failed to recognize was that a healthy party system as opposed to a court (the corrupt Walpolian regime) and a country interest (the nation at large) could, with its proper parliamentary system of checks and balances, be of inestimable benefit to a nation. Hammond writes:

> Such a view [court versus country] inhibited the necessary growth of institutionalized opposition because it was based on the premise that a perfectly functioning government would command universal approbation. Opposition, to Bolingbroke, was a desperate remedy that could only be justified in a state of national emergency, when the constitution and civil liberty were endangered. The opponent of government was either a 'Patriot', selflessly acting in his country's interest, or he was a factionalist and a danger to the body politic.[30]

Was Bolingbroke being sincere in his belief in the nonexistence of parties, asserting that the true division was between constitutionalists and anti-constitutionalists, or was this simply 'part of a campaign to deny the reality of party differences which were obstructing his own advancement'[31]? This brings up the question of the relationship between political ideology and political practice. Namier and his school are convinced that there is no connection between the two, politics (in the eighteenth century) being merely a frantic quest for office and power. Others such as Skinner, Mansfield and Kramnick have viewed Bolingbroke's political creed as being the result of long-held principles and the desire to stem the rising tide of corruption which could put the nation's freedom in jeopardy. The inconsistencies of his own political conduct which have unquestionably lessened his political reputation as a statesman and theorist should perhaps be placed in the context of his own paradoxicality and that of the fallibility of human nature. He was, at the very least, a most perceptive analyst who could see and report the most significant constitutional developments of his age. Without finding any specific remedies for the situation he deplored (save vague appeals to the ancient constitution, the balance of powers, and the spirit of patriotism and liberty), he noted 'the breakdown of the old party distinctions and the revival of Court and Country as the essential political dichotomy, the important shift in the balance of economic and political power as a consequence of the financial revolution, and the threat to the balanced constitution, to the independence of Parliament and to the liberty of the nation posed by the expansion of the central administration, the increase in the number of placemen and the growing power of royal ministers'[32].

It may well have been, as Fletcher persuasively points out[33], that Bolingbroke's lengthy residence in France gave him not only a considerable knowledge of the disheartening political situation but also a greater understanding of the history of France and French institutions. As a result his awareness of the difference between the two countries was considerably heightened, making his pleas for liberty and stability much more cogent. In no way must England fall into the misery of tyrannical despotism where men become enslaved without redress. Unlike some of the more optimistic philosophes, he had little faith in any improvement in France and became considerably more pessimistic in his views about England after lengthy exposure to French government. However, the ever-receding hope of personal advancement was a considerable factor in his increasingly gloomy outlook. Alary, Pouilly and Vertot had taught him much about the nature and history of French society. Despotism was unknown in the distant past; men lived by fundamental laws and had a voice in government as a result of a free contract between the sovereign and themselves. How they had lost this was a matter of conjecture and there were many differing opinions as to the way it could be restored. The struggle in France for a more representative government, for the curbing of the despotic royal power and for the revival of France's ancient Gothic constitution with its attendant liberties, was used by Bolingbroke on his return to England to give additional substance to

67

his war against the Walpolian regime. Though his view
of the Roman legacy to both England and France was
rather inconsistent[34], he never lost his fascination
for the Roman republic whose greatness depended on its
citizens' freedom and the wise balance of
constitutional power. Vertot confirmed him in this
view, and Montesquieu was to develop it later[35].
Boulainvilliers, with whom Bolingbroke had many
fruitful discussions, appears to have held very
similar views to those of Bolingbroke, as a comparison
of the <u>Histoire de l'ancien gouvernement de la France</u>
and the <u>Remarks on the History of England</u> shows. Both
urge a return of the ancient spirit of the
Constitution and condemn the evils of despotic power
which was alien to the character of both nations.
Here again however, we can note further
inconsistencies in Bolingbroke's thought patterns, for
in many of his pamphlets he was fond of pointing out
that England had a monopoly on liberty right from
earliest times unlike France which had never really
experienced truly democratic institutions, a point of
view heartily echoed by Chesterfield and Horace
Walpole later.

The idea of a patriot King or Prince who would be
a limited or constitutional ruler guaranteeing the
liberties of his people and acting in their best
interest was not a new one either in England or in
France. Bossuet wrote two works for his royal pupil,
in one of which (<u>Politique tirée de l'histoire sainte</u>)
he expressed the view that monarchy was the best form
of government, but that the King must follow the law
of God (Bolingbroke's natural law) and base his
actions on love and charity. His famous <u>Discours sur
l'histoire universelle</u> was written specifically to
influence the conduct of a royal leader and make him a
patriot King. Following Bossuet, Fénelon,
Boulainvilliers and Ramsay had stressed the crying
need for a responsible and benevolent ruler who would
consult his country's needs. Voltaire, Montesquieu
and most of the <u>philosophes</u> were in complete agreement
that this type of active, constitutional and moral
leader was exactly what France required. It was
important however to build safeguards into this
monarchical system since a ruler, no matter how ideal
he might appear, was a fallible human being.
Bolingbroke had been very much impressed, while in
France, with the struggles of the 'parlements' to
recover their ancient rights as an intermediary
between King and nation, and to exercise an important

and responsible role in the legislation and in the expression of public opinion in political affairs. In several articles of the <u>Craftsman</u>, he suggests that the English could well follow the example of the French in arousing a spirit of patriotism among the people to help them stand up against tyranny, although they did not have to contend with the despotism of a King or a Church as in France. What riled Bolingbroke and many of his peers (Lord Chesterfield for one) was that while the English parliament was basically infinitely superior to the French 'parlements', its members had become spineless, abject minions of the government. Thus, while condemning the political situation in France as a whole, Bolingbroke was well aware of the efforts of the French to shake off their yoke and used this knowledge in his attacks on his own government. The various 'remontrances' of the French 'parlements' may well have provided some of the inspiration for the <u>Patriot King</u>.

There is no doubt that Bolingbroke's political works had a considerable impact in France where his generalizations about the basic principles of government were warmly received by thinkers and writers vitally concerned about the enslaved condition of the French people. Articles from the <u>Craftsman</u> (in particular the <u>Dissertation Upon Parties</u>) had appeared in French translation as early as the 30's, and Bolingbroke's impressive rhetoric on the constant theme of corruption with many examples taken from the France of Cardinal de Richelieu would have galvanized his French readers. His <u>Remarks on the History of England</u>, written in 1730-31, was translated in 1743 but had already been consulted by Voltaire in preparing his <u>Lettres philosophiques</u> which appeared first in English translation in 1733. His letter to Sir William Wyndham translated as the <u>Mémoires secrets</u> appeared in 1754 with its analysis of English politics from 1710 to 1716 and French intrigues during the author's stay in France in 1717, and the <u>Lettres sur l'esprit de patriotisme, sur l'idée d'un roi patriote et sur l'état des partis qui divisaient l'Angleterre lors de l'avènement de George Ier</u>, published in 1750, were immensely popular and influential in France, all the more as the author had drawn on his considerable political experience in both countries. The universal concepts of liberty, stability, virtue, and happiness bound together widely different minds, transcending national and religious barriers.

There is no question that Voltaire's view of England as expressed in the Lettres Philosophiques was largely influenced by the many discussions he had had with Bolingbroke in France and in England and by the expression of the latter's thought in his various articles and publications. In the letters on the Parliament, Voltaire takes up the themes of venality and corruption of members, the idea of opposition, completely unknown as a political ploy in France, the notion of a King who is prevented from wrong-doing by the contract between him and the people, the theory of mixed government with its system of checks and balances (balance of power), and the view that England is the champion of European liberty and will go to war to promote it, unlike countries such as France, Turkey and Spain which seek revenge on one tyrant only to fall into the clutches of another. All these ideas can be found in The Craftsman, though other sources such as Bayle, Fénelon (Télémaque), Rapin de Thoyras, Lenglet-Dufresnoy, and English papers like The Gentleman's Magazine, Fog's Weekly Journal, The London Journal, The Free Briton may well have been tapped. As Lanson points out[36], the fact that Voltaire was working on this eighth letter in July of 1732 when The Craftsman issue of July 22 was published, gives strong support to the question of Bolingbroke's influence on his political thought. In the ninth letter on Government, Voltaire's main theme on the origins of the English constitution seems to be largely derived from The Craftsman, though other works such as the History of the High Court of Parliament, Algernon Sidney's Discourses concerning government, Temple's Introduction to the History of England, Roger Acherley's Britannic Constitution and Rapin de Thoyras' Histoire de l'Angleterre were put to good use. Voltaire disagreed with the Whig view of the antiquity of the English constitution and its liberties, following rather the Tory line that an historic evolution, assisted often by force, was responsible for the present state of English liberty and for the power of the Commons. Bolingbroke shared both views, admitting a spirit of freedom inherited from England's Germanic and French past, but proclaiming that the free institutions of England were the laborious results of a struggle against secular and ecclesiastical tyranny ('La liberté est née en Angleterre des querelles des tyrans'[37]). The idea that, after the Norman conquest which reduced the nation to slavery, the clashes between the Kings, the powerful Barons and the Clergy were instrumental in providing the goundwork for a more equal free

70

government, is specific in both Bolingbroke and Voltaire[38]. The <u>Magna Charta</u> which vastly improved the condition of the people was thus the accidental effect of these rivalries, an excellent example of how the course of history can be changed by the unforeseen. Voltaire's remarks on commerce in the tenth letter could have been gleaned from many sources as well as from his own observations. The idea that by trade and commerce England became a rich and powerful nation appears many times in Bolingbroke's works and would certainly have been impressed on Voltaire's mind in their various discussions; the corollary that the wealth accumulated was one of the factors in establishing English freedom is implicit in contemporary writings, explicit in Voltaire[39]. What particularly impressed him was the fact that, unlike France, England held its merchants in the greatest respect; far from being demeaning for the relatives of peers of the realm, commerce and industry were worthy professions, infinitely more useful than the petty and senseless occupations of a powdered French aristocrat, 'jouant le rôle d'esclave dans l'antichambre d'un Ministre'[40]. The future patriarch of Ferney was to put these lessons to great profit when directing his farms and industries, enriching himself and others and achieving the independence that he had admired in England.

In treating the influence of Bolingbroke on Voltaire's political credo, it must not be forgotten that, even before the latter's visit to England, he was well acquainted with other important figures such as Prior and Lord Stair and had read widely in the field of political journalism. All in all his view of England as expressed in the <u>Lettres philosophiques</u> and in his articles in the <u>Dictionnaire philosophique</u>, was a limited one colored by his friendship with important aristocrats like Bolingbroke. The nation appears as a particular and superficial segment of society rather than a microcosm of opposing and contradictory aspirations and desires. He did not see the abuses and the injustices that often made the life of the masses so miserable; for them freedom was merely an abstraction which they could never hope to realize. His political ideal was that of the English system of government, aristocratic, democratic and monarchical, and his views changed little during the course of a long life. All his energies were spent in attacking tyranny in whatever form it might appear and in eulogizing independence of thought and political freedom. While both he and Bolingbroke stressed the important role of Parliament as an intermediary between King and nation, he was not fettered by the imperious demands of personal ambition which led Bolingbroke to concentrate all his venomous criticism on the despotism of one particular minister, becoming, in fact, so obsessed in later life, that he appeared convinced English liberties were doomed and the Constitution was committed to the irreversible process of decay[41]. Ill-health as well as disappointed hopes may well have contributed to this pessimistic view, and during the natural reaction in France to the often expressed notion of the perfect English nation, these later criticisms were used to good advantage by French patriots who were planning optimistically for a new French society. England was not to be envied so much after all. It is to Voltaire's credit that he appeared to be unaffected by Bolingbroke's pessimism; England to him would always be the land of freedom. Thus they both had evolved but in rather different directions. Bolingbroke's early facile optimism, criticized by a more cynical Voltaire in Candide particularly, had turned into a difficult pessimism, while Voltaire finally reached the plateau of a rational optimism: this was in fact the best of all possible worlds.

The personal and intellectual relations between Bolingbroke and Montesquieu have been studied by a number of critics including Joseph Dedieu, Robert Shackleton, and Dennis Fletcher, and all have come to the conclusion, based on a careful analysis of the writings of both, that Bolingbroke exercised a powerful influence on Montesquieu's thought, especially as it is expressed in the Esprit des Lois. Before his visit to England (1729-31), Montesquieu had already met a number of distinguished statesmen and diplomats - Horatio Walpole, Lord Waldegrave, Lord Townshend, the Duke of Berwick and Lord Chesterfield, Ambassador at The Hague, to whom he presented a letter of introduction from Waldegrave and on whose yacht he travelled to England. Chesterfield and Montesquieu became firm friends and lifelong correspondents, and there is little doubt that politics would have been the main topic of interest. Since this correspondence is no longer extant, it is impossible to assess the undoubted influence which Chesterfield exerted in the formulation of his friend's English education. As can be seen by an analysis of the Lettres persanes, Montesquieu was already fascinated by the English concept of liberty[42] and had read widely in the field of English political thought[43]. His English sojourn was the most important period of his life, though strangely enough one of the most obscure. There is almost complete silence in English newspapers, no mention in the letters of Pope and Chesterfield or the memoirs of Lord Hervey, and his English journal which would have thrown significant light on his experiences and thoughts was burned by his grandson in England. His knowledge of English was adequate; he had taken lessons in English while in Italy and had studied sundry grammars and text-books. While he never achieved complete fluency, he was able to understand the spoken language and could read easily. Bolingbroke may have met Montesquieu in the salon of the Marquise de Lambert or at the home of mutual friends such as Matignon and Berwick. His future wife, the Marquise de Villette, was known to Montesquieu as early as 1722, while in a letter to Warburton in 1752, Montesquieu affirms that he had first met Bolingbroke in that same year[44]. We have seen that both had attended meetings at the <u>Club de l'Entresol</u> whereMontesquieu would have learned a great deal from Bolingbroke about international politics and the English system in particular. The relationship was not as warm or close as that between the French author and Chesterfield, despite Dedieu's belief that they were intimate and 'faits pour s'entendre'[45]. The few references to Bolingbroke in the <u>Pensées et fragments inédits</u>, in the <u>Spicilège</u> and in the <u>Correspondance</u> are proof enough that Montesquieu considered him brilliant but immoral (therefore a very pernicious influence), admirable for his oratory and persuasiveness but unworthy of esteem, a man who had betrayed both public and private interests and whose fiery eloquence was directed against people and things intemperately[46]. Bolingbroke was equally antipathetic, and it appears that their personal relationship ceased after Montesquieu returned to France in 1731, or even before while he was still in England, 'sans qu'aucun de nous deux s'en aperçût' as Montesquieu himself puts it[47].

Nonetheless, Montesquieu was wise enough to profit by the undoubted political sagacity of Bolingbroke in the immense plan that was already firmly implanted in his mind, that of writing a major work on the study of laws. Three years after his return to France, he had published (anonymously at Amsterdam) his <u>Considérations sur les causes de la</u>

grandeur des Romains et de leur décadence which was originally to have been the first chapter of the Esprit des Lois and which was to inspire Gibbon's great work. He had heard parallels between the greatness of the Roman empire and the noble British Constitution frequently discussed in the political circles and salons he had frequented in England, particularly that of his great friend Chesterfield, himself so steeped in the lore of antiquity, and in articles by Pulteney and Bolingbroke in The Craftsman which he avidly read. Both Bolingbroke and Montesquieu had read widely in the literature of antiquity, particularly the works of Polybius and Cicero, and derived many of their political ideas (eg. notion of liberty, balance of power) from them. The eminent Marlborough was compared by the Whigs to the greatest Roman generals, and Addison had produced his Roman tragedy, Cato, in 1713. Many scholars, imbued with the aspirations and ideas of the past, were appalled at the sight of unbridled luxury which seemed to be gaining prevalence in English society and longed for a return to the spirit of moderation and frugality which had made Rome great. Both Montesquieu and Bolingbroke had witnessed the same tendency towards intemperate frivolity in France's Regency period, though they had also been a party to the numerous political controversies that often monopolized social life in the salons, clubs and academies. The Roman concept of virtus which combined the notions of moral virtue and virile action was one which strongly appealed to both men, and it colored many of their political views. The reason for the decadence of Roman civilization was the gradual loss of this virtus leading to corruption in government and public and private immorality. Passions such as immoderate ambition, avarice, envy and jealousy eroded the national spirit, resulting in political and moral lethargy, poverty of mind and body, and finally the loss of that precious liberty that was their birthright. Enslaved politically, mentally and morally, the Romans were no match for the barbaric hordes that swept down from the North. The lessons to be learned had of course been pointed out by others such as Fénelon whose Aventures de Télémaque, written towards 1695, had caused quite a stir in both France and England. The fictitious land of Bétique and the Kingdom of Salente symbolized the yearnings of noble minds for a return to the purity of first principles.

The Roman model thus provided the link between politics and morality to which both writers strongly adhere. Laws can be effective only as long as the people for whom they are made act as moral and responsible citizens. Since both men were realists, it followed that there was no guarantee of either situation. Though they both lauded the English Constitution as their political ideal, they knew from experience that there had been a marked deterioration in political life since the halcyon days of 1688. If human nature is fallible, and no one denies it, then decay of some form or another will be inevitable. Both men were conservative in their dislike of change the inevitability of which in any society they failed to appreciate. The idea of progress in the Enlightenment sense with the notion of optimism that accompanied it was alien to them, as too was the idea of political revolution. The solution for both rested in the restoration <u>in spirit</u> of the Revolution of 1688 which still allegedly controlled the English political situation. It was the spirit or the character of a nation that must prevail; without this all the best laid plans and laws would come to naught. How far Montesquieu's <u>esprit général</u> is an echo of Bolingbroke's <u>English spirit</u> is uncertain, though the <u>Remarks on the History of England</u> in which it appears were well-known to the French author. The expression appears in Rapin de Thoyras' <u>Histoire d'Angleterre</u> published some years before, a work that both had read carefully. As we have seen, the idea if not explicitly expressed, is already in embryonic form in the <u>Lettres persanes</u> published before either the <u>Remarks</u> or the <u>Histoire</u>.

While both Bolingbroke and Montesquieu were in accord on the notion of a stable constitution with fixed laws as the only certain way to stem the tide of inevitable corruption and degeneration, they fully realized that it would have to vary in nature depending on the needs and situation of different peoples. The natural genius must be consulted, or else no laws would be effective in guaranteeing liberty and happiness. The principle of relativity was thus recognized as being immensely important in the elaboration of a suitable constitution for each different nation. What Montesquieu refers to as <u>les moeurs</u> is not exactly translated as morals <u>or</u> customs (it can of course mean both) in the political context. It is more accurately defined as <u>habitudes d'une société on d'un individu relatives à la pratique du bien et du mal</u>, a definition which gives politics both

a social and an ethical sense. This was the view of
Bolingbroke and also that of Voltaire (_Essai sur les
moeurs_). There were of course conditions, different
in different countries, affecting these habits of
people, conditions such as geography and climate which
had to be taken into account when adapting a
constitution to the national character. Their role in
determining the _moeurs_ was paramount, and much harm
could be done by ignoring them. Bolingbroke explains,
but does not dilate upon this point in his _Patriot
King_, having in mind particularly the unstable climate
of insular Britain which may well account for the
fickle nature of the English. Montesquieu develops the
idea to its fullest extent, studying the law in its
relations with the nature of government, climate and
terrain, with the principles which form the _esprit
général_, and with the _moeurs_ and _manières_ of a nation.
Machiavelli, whose works were much in fashion in the
first half of the eighteenth century, could have
suggested to both writers the importance of climate on
national character, the social implications of civil
government, and the cyclical nature of history, though
his advocacy of expediency rather than morality in
political affairs was rejected by them. It is more
than probable, as Shackleton suggests[48], that
Montesquieu's early interest in Machiavelli, suspended
after examination of this unscrupulous view, was
rekindled as a result of articles in _The Craftsman_
(especially June 13 and June 27, 1730) which served to
remind him that the author of the _Discorsi_ was indeed
a more valuable source than he had once thought.

Both Montesquieu and Bolingbroke were fatalistic
in their views on government, which was partly a
result of their determinist theories of the inexorable
outside forces that affected human conduct and over
which man had no control. Though they believed that
man was born morally good, they did not deny evil
existed in the world, and man, together with the
institutions he sought to establish, would ineluctably
be corrupted by it, consciously or unconsciously. The
notion of the vicious circle where the government is
corrupted by evil ministers who in turn corrupt the
people, and where the prince, who initially was the
servant of the public, becomes a dictator to the
public is found in the writings of both. An influence
cannot be successfully established here, since this
had been a common concept in Locke[49] and repeated in

contemporary writing by Swift in his dissertation on the fatal consequences of dissension between the nobles and the Commons in Athens and Rome. Interestingly, both writers take the view that man's bad instincts can be put to good effect in the realm of politics. This was simply a corollary of Fontenelle's theory of the importance of studying past errors in order to arrive at a proper understanding of the truth. Freedom was the ideal of all three, physical, mental, moral and political. Before his visit to England, at about the time when he published the _Lettres persanes_ (1721), Montesquieu's view of political liberty had been equivocal. Provided that a people were immune from deprivation by arbitrary means of life and property, he could see no real advantage in a free state as opposed to a tyrannical one. Shortly after, his meeting with Bolingbroke, his discussions in the _Entresol_, and particularly his stay in England where he was a welcome guest at the most important houses and at debates in the House of Commons (he was, it appears, a fascinated witness of democratic Parliamentary procedure[50]), caused a radical change in his views. By the time the _Considérations_ were published in 1734, he was fully convinced that liberty was rather the product of wise laws than the favor bestowed by a benevolent monarch. His essay on the English Constitution, written in 1733 and modified in 1748 to form chapter 6 of Book XI of the _Esprit des Lois_, is a well-reasoned and balanced account of the government as seen through English eyes. In the belief that liberty was attainable only by going back to first principles which must perforce be virtuous, honorable, vigorous and efficient, Montesquieu is echoing not only Bolingbroke's views in _The Craftsman_ which in turn echoed those of Algernon Sidney (_Discourses concerning government_, 1704), but the famous solution of Machiavelli in the _Discorsi_:

E cosa più chiara che la luce, che non si rinnuovando questi corpi, non durano. Il modo di rinnuovarli è ... ridurli verso i principj suoi.[51]

Montesquieu's theory of government was influenced by a simplification of Aristotle (division of government into monarchy, aristocracy and democracy) and Polybius (the idea of the mixed state), by Plélo, whose paper at a meeting of the _Entresol_ on monarchical and other forms of government created widespread interest, by Machiavelli (republic and monarchy classified as good governments, tyranny as bad), by Hobbes and Spinoza (the doctrine of the preservation of one's own nature as being good and healthy), by Paolo Doria (insistence on the three modes of life which are independent of the three different forms of government, la barbara, la civile moderata, la civile pomposa), by Bolingbroke (who argued there must be good in the first principle of all governments or they could not subsist at all), and by Pope (whatever is best administered is best) as well as by numerous other writers and thinkers. But his systematic political treatise was quite new in European thought. After claiming that each government has its own nature, principle and object, he subdivides the republic into democracy, where the sovereign power resides in the hands of the people, and aristocracy, where it resides in the hands of only a portion of the people. What concerns him is not the location of power but the way it is used. Monarchy was in his view the best form and despotism the worst. Liberty was the keynote of Montesquieu's political theory, liberty which depended on the harmonious relationship between forms and customs and the spirit or character of the nation. The role of Parliament as custodian and interpreter of the laws was paramount in securing this freedom since it stood between the monarch, who, one hoped, would put the interests of his people first but without any certain guarantee, and the nation which needed responsible guidance moral and political. This liberty once gained or restored in the case of France, would produce a virtuous nation. In Chapter V of Book XI, Montesquieu wisely sidesteps the issue of whether the English have achieved liberty or not, contenting himself with declaring that their wise laws had established it in principle. Parliament, however, was not the only intermediary power between the Crown and the people. Writing in the French context where the tendency towards royal despotism was becoming more and more marked, Montesquieu gives cardinal importance to the role of the nobility who possessed a judicial function and the clergy whose notorious privileges, though intrinsically unjust, would serve to balance and restrain royal power.

Already, in his Grandeur et Décadence des Romains, Montesquieu had outlined what he was to develop later as his famous separation of powers. He refers in the second volume to the harmonious union between all parts of a political body as being essential to the well-being of society despite or perhaps because of their very disparate nature. An analogy is drawn with music where dissonances can neutralize one another and lead to perfect harmony (be it only in the ear of the listener!). And just as great music is divinely inspired, so should the ideal constitution reflect the moral order of God's universe. Much controversy has resulted from the question of Bolingbroke's influence on Montesquieu in the formulation of his theory of power separation, and indeed it was a knotty problem in the English political world of the day. The two rival journals (The London Journal and The Craftsman) waged a real battle over the notions of independence and interdependence of powers, the former hotly denying that any effective government could be carried out by powers distinct and absolutely independent. The latter reflected Bolingbroke's view that the whole depended on the balance of the parts and the balance of the parts on their mutual independence. Montesquieu, who keenly followed this battle (which took place during his visit), may have thought, with the London Journal, that Bolingbroke was advocating a strict separation of the legislative and executive powers. The latter came close to this at times, but his ideas were often inconsistent and confused. In general he described the sharing of these two functions by the three estates (King, Lords, Commons), but feared that if the independence of Parliament were to be threatened by royal abuse a loss of liberty would result. A proper balance between the three ensured that no one estate could subvert the authority of the others, thus maintaining a mutual independence within the framework of this political equilibrium. As Pocock has clearly pointed out, Bolingbroke's concept of independence 'must be interpreted as meaning, not encroachment by one jurisdiction upon another, but corruption occurring when "indirect influence" made the members of one governing body personally dependent upon another; as talking, not the language of the function, but that of morality'[52]. What Bolingbroke firmly believed in was a mixed constitution in which the three estates would co-operate to their mutual benefit and that of the nation at large. This co-operation entailed a constitutional dependency, while their right to inviolacy which had to be preserved at any cost constituted a mutual independence. Montesquieu's theory of the separation of powers may well have been stimulated by the English controversy, but it was not taken in the form he expressed it from Bolingbroke[53].

79

In his pleas for a separation of the legislature and the executive, Bolingbroke was directly attacking the Walpole brothers who, by bribery and corruption (which they considered a necessary governmental expedient), were unduly increasing their executive authority to the point where as ministers they were tending to become despotic, forcing parliament to bow to their wills. The legislative authority vested in the three estates needed to be shared in a way that would maintain an equilibrium of power that was guaranteed by the English constitution and essential to the liberty of the nation. The situation in France was of course, as both Bolingbroke and Montesquieu were aware, quite different. With an absolute monarchy, the Parlements had been dominated and overridden to such an extent that they possessed no real influence and were waging a constant struggle to assert their time-honored rights. The case for separation of the executive and legislative in the English context resulted from the establishment of the new post of prime minister of which Walpole was the first occupant and from his use of cabinet councils, and Montesquieu did not fail to notice the danger of legislative and executive functions resting in the hands of one man. This was one of the dangers inherent in the limited monarchy system, but on the whole, the English system was remediable within the working of the Constitution unlike the despotic government that obtained in France. Parliaments, which in both Bolingbroke's and Montesquieu's view were guardians of liberty, had to be incorruptible; for this to happen, the people, guided by the true spirit of patriotism, had to elect members of moral and political integrity. The notion of a patriotic King lost its urgency in Bolingbroke's mind with the passage of time, and his hopes for a regeneration of the constitution receded visibly in his later years, while Montesquieu's optimism (though he shared Bolingbroke's fear about England's future) remained relatively unshaken. The genius of the English people would ensure that, somehow or other, their freedom would be assured despite the corruption of the government officials. This was more or less Bolingbroke's view earlier as expressed in the Dissertation upon Parties[54]. His idea of annual Parliamentary elections and particularly the danger of standing armies as having different interests and loyalties than the rest of the nation and a possible hot bed therefore of faction, finds an echo in the Esprit des Lois[55], as does the question of excessive taxation the evils of which were only too apparent in

France. Cuttings Montesquieu made from The Craftsman were carefully pinned into his note-book, incontrovertible evidence of his deep interest in the lessons that France could learn from the English Constitution. His famous work, though influential in both France and England after its publication (1748), suffered an eclipse towards 1760 when French opinion reacted against the close links he had forged between politics and morality (liberty did not necessarily produce virtue, it was said); when a wave of anglophobia swept in about the same period, it turned against the whole concept of liberty in the English sense as an idle notion devoid of all political value. The era of Rousseau was at hand.

Despite the obvious dissimilarites of temperament and thought between Bolingbroke and Rousseau, there is reason to believe that the latter shared some of the English statesmen's political views. It is unlikely that they ever met nor is there any reference in the works and correspondence of either. Yet they had a mutual acquaintance in the Abbé de Saint-Pierre and in Mme Dupin whose salon they both visited, though at different times[56]. The latter could well have been an intermediary between Bolingbroke, who was by no means reluctant in pronouncing on the sorry state of England and on his remedies for it, and Rousseau who became her secretary in 1746. The contribution of Rousseau to the history of European thought is far greater than that of Bolingbroke or even Montesquieu; his sweep was much wider and, in the words of Cazamian, 'he had much more of the future in him than of the past'[57]. While it may well be safer to stress affinity rather than influence in the case of Rousseau, he has undoubted similarities with Bolingbroke. Compared to the Contrat Social, Bolingbroke's political reflections and even Montesquieu's Esprit des Lois seem severely limited and unsatisfactory. Rousseau handles the complexities of the subject with a logical and yet passionate mind, showing all the instincts of a visionary in his zeal for justice and equality. Once again the influence of Machiavelli can be seen in the Contrat Social as it has been noted in the case of Bolingbroke and Montesquieu, especially in the idea of Le législateur, the benevolent and wise leader who by the force of his personality will effect a moral regeneration of the people. Both Bolingbroke and Rousseau stressed the almost superhuman qualities which this leader, divinely inspired, had to have - intelligence, understanding, compassion, realism and idealism at the same time - and he had to educate his people by the force of his own example. In addition he must act in conformity with the moeurs, the customs, and the spirit of the laws; public opinion was a very important force in society and politics and had to be carefully nurtured. The collective soul of a nation and the spirit of patriotism are the most important considerations; even bad legislation would not corrupt citizens if the moral quality of the nation remained inviolate. Yet Bolingbroke, whose view of politics was more practical than Rousseau's, was under no illusion that these ideas were Utopian and plain wishful thinking[58].

As an organ of public opinion, The Craftsman exerted a powerful influence in France. We have seen that both Voltaire and Montesquieu read and made extracts from it while in England and after their return to France. For those whose knowledge of English was non-existent or minimal, a translation of several numbers was made in 1737 (published in Amsterdam) by a certain Le Cène who attests to its immense popularity. French statesmen and diplomats were able to consult this version which must have circulated clandestinely in France since, as a torch of liberty, it could have set afire the smouldering resentments of the French nation. Comparisons must have been made between the free press of England and the strict censorship that obtained in France. D'Argenson and his fellow Ministers were fearful in 1751 that 'un vent philosophique du gouvernement libre et anti-monarchique' would have disastrous effects in France, though philosophic milieus welcomed it as a harbinger of better things to come[59]. Articles in the translation of 1737 dealing with such things as a servile press and theatre, bribery, standing armies, excessive taxes, the idea of popular liberty and free democratic government as a nation's right not privilege, the appeals to reason divinely bestowed, the criticisms of the divine right of Kings and infallibility, and the concept of a wise, just and good sovereign whose duty was to watch over the actions of his ministers and the interests of his people, were eagerly read, assimilated, and hotly discussed in the salons of the day. In other numbers there are covert or overt comparisons between the English and French political systems to the obvious advantage of the former. Though none of the 1737 issues were directly from the pen of Bolingbroke who was at this time in exile in France, he was still the driving force behind the scenes and would have continued to monitor the material that was to appear. For all those struggling against a repressive regime, The Craftsman sent out a welcome ray of hope.

Apart from great names such as Montesquieu and Voltaire, many lesser lights in France acted consciously or unconsciously as porte-parole of Bolingbroke. Some were primarily translators of his works, Etienne de Silhouette, Minister of Finances and an anglophile who had a warm personal relationship with Bolingbroke and who translated not only the Dissertation upon Parties in 1739, but also some of Pope's works (Essay on Man, Essay on Criticism)[60], Charles Le Cène (already mentioned as translator of The Craftsman, June-December 1737), J. Barbeu du Bourg (Letter to Sir William Wyndham, Letters on the Study and Use of History, Reflections on Exile, On the True Use of Retirement and Study), Claude de Thyard, Comte de Bissy (Letters on the Spirit of Patriotism; on the idea of a Patriot-King ; on the State of the Parties at the Accession of George I), J.L. Favier (A Letter to Sir William Wyndham, published as Mémoires secrets de Mylord Bolingbroke), the Abbé Le Blanc and Mauvillon (Some Reflections on the Present State of the Nation), and those who preferred to remain anonymous. Others were authors - David Durand who completed Rapin de Thoyras' Histoire d'Angleterre, the thirteenth volume of which deals with the Bolingbroke administration and echoes many of his favorite political and historical themes, and the Marquis d'Argenson (Journal et Mémoires).

The latter two names typify the aspect of Bolingbroke's influence which did nothing whatever to stimulate admiration for England's political constitution. It is one of the tragedies of his life that Bolingbroke should have become so obsessed by the idea of the political disintegration of the English nation, throwing off pamphlet after pamphlet of damaging criticism, that he became one of the main authorities for those anxious to denigrate the democratic system that was the cause of England's woes in favor of a political remedy which would be more suitable for France's needs. Yet even here, one could say that the Bolingbroke paradox stimulated thought and led to positive action which, however different from that which he had originally expounded, was to lead the nation from the dark tunnel of serfdom to the light of freedom. He was not alone in despairing of a solution to his country's problems, though with his

83

usual penchant for extremes, his language became quite intemperate at times[61]. His contemporary, Lord Chesterfield, albeit of the opposite party, wrote to Marchmont in 1741 that he preferred to converse 'with the cheerful, natural born slaves of France, than with the sullen, venal, voluntary ones of England'[62]. The concept of patriotism so lauded by Bolingbroke had seized hold on the French imagination in a way that he would never have suspected. His uncomplimentary remarks on the English nation as expressed in The Craftsman and in his numerous works influenced French patriots who were anxious to restore their own genius and show its superiority over the overrated English spirit. In the Archives of the Quai d'Orsay there exist many copies of The Craftsman where the worst features of the English political system are described and lamented. These aspects colored the judgment of State Ministers and influenced the direction of foreign policy in many subtle ways. France had no need to fear a neighboring nation whose moral and political fibre was so low. As Fletcher justly comments, the Marquis d'Argenson exploited this view in order to convince public opinion 'that the pattern of English political life could not be adapted to suit French needs, and that benevolent and enlightened despotism was really the answer to their country's problems'. D'Argenson becomes quite carried away when pursuing this theme, to the point where he treats the balance of power and mixed government in England as reasons for England's degeneration. This view, based on the 1737 translation of The Craftsman, was later modified when he became Minister of Foreign Affairs (1747). He clearly saw then that Parliament was in reality the force to be reckoned with in England and that its ability to curb the royal power was real and not imagined[63]. The Abbé Le Blanc (Lettres d'un Français, 1745), who was at first a convinced anglophile, appears to have become very disillusioned at the spectacle of English politics, while Genest lashed out venomously at England in a number of works the most significant of which is the periodical Etat politique actuel de l'Angleterre (1757-59, 10 vols). According to Dedieu, Genest was 'le vulgarisateur parfait de la haine anglaise', and his views were enthusiastically endorsed by his English disciple, Brown, whose Estimate of the Manners and Principles of the Times (1757) was translated by Chais and enjoyed an immense popularity in both England and France[64]. More famous figures such as Diderot and d'Holbach may well have been instrumental in propagating this pessimistic view of England, though the latter would also have had many opportunities of hearing the praises of the Walpolian regime from Sir Robert's son, Horace[65].

CONCLUSION

CRITICAL OPINION

Critical opinion in both England and France has been sharply divided since Bolingbroke's death in 1751, and particularly after the posthumous publication of his works by Mallet in 1754. During his lifetime he had been highly praised in both countries as a brilliant orator, writer and statesman, but severely condemned (in England rather than in France) for his personal immorality and proved treachery toward his country and some of his friends (Marlborough, Harley, Pope). Once his charismatic personality was no longer present to dazzle and cloud men's judgments, and the public was allowed to sample his complete works, a very different reaction set in. His best friends remained loyal to him. To Pope he was the greatest man who ever lived, and he remained a very dear memory to Swift who kept to himself his reservations about Bolingbroke's personal character. His contemporary, Chesterfield, though a Whig and critical of his political conduct and defects of character, held him up to his son as a brilliant example of a man who, by his exquisite breeding, rhetoric and gracious manners, had reached the peak of political eminence, an ideal which the fond parent had always set before his son and later his godson. In a letter to Mme de Monconseil, nine months after his death, Chesterfield wrote:

> Quel homme! Quelle étendue de connaissances! Quelle mémoire! Quelle éloquence! Ses passions qui étaient fortes, faisaient tort à la délicatesse de ses sentiments; on les confondait, et souvent exprès: on lui rendra justice à présent, qu'on ne lui en a rendu de son vivant.[66]

Lord Hervey was much less generous, though he found some good qualities:

> He had fine talents, a natural eloquence, great quickness, a happy memory, and very extensive knowledge: but he was vain -- timid, false, injudicious, and ungrateful; elate and insolent in power, dejected and servile in disgrace -- ambitious without fortitude, and enterprising without resolution; -- fawning without insinuation, and insincere without art -- he had admirers without friendship, and followers

without attachment; parts without probity, knowledge without conduct, and experience without judgement.[67]

Horace Walpole disliked him intensely (he was an archfiend and a mock patriot)[68], and never forgave him for his long opposition to his beloved father, Sir Robert. Chesterfield proved to be wrong in his prognostications, for his reputation fared even more badly after 1754. This was due partly to the paradoxical nature of his temperament and life (even Chesterfield was appalled by the 'sudden contrast' between his virtues and vices, his reason and his passions, remembering also, no doubt, Bolingbroke's comments on the powerlessness of the most exalted human reason)[69], and partly to the inconsistencies and occasional incoherences of his moral and political philosophy. William Pitt and Lady Mary Wortley Montagu were disappointed at his lack of originality and his superficiality, while the latter went so far as to accuse him of plagiarism.[70] Dr. Johnson, ever the sour grapes, considered him a scoundrel who was cowardly enough not to publish his controversial works in his lifetime.[71] Curiously enough, Horace Walpole was vituperated after his own death for organizing a posthumous publication of his highly critical <u>Memoirs</u>. Yet it was a feature of the times, when censorship was so rigorous, that many authors both in England and in France chose to write anonymously or pseudonymously, to publish posthumously or to arrange clandestine publications of their works, often with foreign presses. What riled most English readers was the propagation of theories of morality and virtue by a writer whose own life was scandalous. And what appeared to be a concerted attack on organised religion aroused critics in both countries. It is probably true to say that Bolingbroke was painfully aware of the effect his views were having on public opinion since some of his letters and essays had been published before his death, and chose to delay publication of the main body of his work in order to escape further attacks. In a way this was understandable considering his past political record, though Dickinson points out that he cannot be excused for undermining, after his death, both Christianity and the Church which he always believed were 'essential bulwarks of the State'.[72]

French readers were alerted to the hue and outcry by better-known scholars such as William Warburton (<u>A View of Lord Bolingbroke's Philosophy</u>), Charles

Bulkeley (<u>Notes on the Philosophical Writings of Lord Bolingbroke</u>), John Leland (<u>Reflections on the late Lord Bolingbroke's Letters on the Study and Use of History</u> and <u>A View of the principal Deistical Writers</u>), and particularly Edmund Burke (<u>Vindication of Natural Society</u>), all of whom were particularly afraid that Bolingbroke's attack on revealed religion would destroy the basis of society as they knew it. Most French critics agreed with these scholars, condemning Bolingbroke's impiety, cowardliness (in a posthumous publication), superficiality, contradictions, and inflated, pretentious rhetoric. Voltaire, as we have seen, had nothing but praise for Bolingbroke's attack on organised religion and superstition, his endorsement of primitive Christian virtues, and his refreshing concept of historical study, but joined with others in the general condemnation of his works. All seemed to agree that his international reputation lent a certain lustre to his writings but that this would quickly dim with the passage of time. The aspect which particularly irritated Voltaire and his fellow critics was the prolixity of his style, a sin which the French with their insistence on <u>le bon goût</u> and their worship of clarity, brevity and method, were loth to forgive.[73] And yet, in many of his tracts, Bolingbroke could write brilliantly, as is evidenced by Chesterfield's comment to his son after reading the <u>Letters on the Spirit of Patriotism</u>. Praising the 'beautiful style', he confessed that he had never before realized 'all the extent and powers of the English language'.[74] This work appeared in a French translation by the Comte de Bissy, but of course the clarity and beauty of the original was lost. However, when a translation appeared in France of his <u>Letters on the Study and Use of History</u> (by Barbeu du Bourg in 1752), not only the ideas but even the style was highly praised.[75]

It seems obvious that Bolingbroke was not at his best in dealing with abstruse philosophical problems. Inconsistency and confusion of thought led to a style that often tended towards convolution. It was as a writer in the fields of history and politics that his reputation remained highest. His encyclopedic knowledge of the English and European political scenes as a result of his own personal involvement enabled him to sketch an inimitable outline in his <u>Letters on the Study and Use of History</u>, particularly of the period between 1659 and 1713. This was the view of Pierre Clément (editor of <u>Les Cinq Années</u>

89

littéraires), of Dr. Maty (writing in <u>Le Journal britannique</u>) who could not resist comparing his account with that of Voltaire in the <u>Siècle de Louis XIV</u>,[76] and of other French reviewers of translations of <u>Craftsman</u> articles that had already appeared in France. Various diplomatic officials such as Chavigny (the French Ambassador), his successor, Bussy, and Silhouette (translator of the <u>Dissertation upon Parties</u>) did a great deal to popularize in France the achievements of such an eminent statesman and writer. Towards 1750, Bolingbroke's political reputation in France appeared to be at its highest point with the appearance of a French translation of <u>Letters on the Spirit of Patriotism</u>. Montesquieu had already recently published his famous <u>Esprit des Lois</u> incorporating many ideas gleaned from Bolingbroke, though his animadversions about his moral character seemed to color his view of him. After that, there was the inevitable decline when the morass of his philosophical opinions engulfed critics on both sides of the Channel. A typical reaction was that of Suard in his <u>Variétés littéraires</u> (1768) where a malicious translation of a defamatory article taken from an English newspaper appeared.[77] So great was the antagonism towards Bolingbroke's ambivalent moral philosophy, often denounced as hypocrisy, that even his historical and political tracts seemed to bear the imprint of his partisan attitude, his overweening arrogance, his bitter misanthropy, and his ineradicable urge to justify his own conduct. Fréron typifies the reactions of most French writers in this respect, criticizing in addition his base treatment of France (supposedly his adopted country and host for many years) in his historical tracts, and the incoherence of much of his work, though he does give Bolingbroke high marks for his undoubted eloquence and imaginative powers.[78] While praising his profound erudition, the author of an article in the <u>Mercure de France</u> of October 1768, devoted to Samuel Pye's attack on Bolingbroke's deism, regretted the error of his ways.[79] What these minor critics in their urge to destroy a man whom they considered an enemy failed to realize, was the important contribution that Bolingbroke had made towards the establishment of a new order in France. He had attempted to reconcile the humanist tradition with the revolutionary ideas of Newton and Locke by attacking the very foundations of orthodox Christianity, inculcating in his readers a sense of man's personal responsibility, proposing a viable scheme of civil government, and holding aloft the torch of freedom which alone could light up man's path to happiness and virtue. Greater figures were more perceptive. Voltaire knew how to appreciate the broad sweep of these ideas so akin to his own, while Montesquieu put to good use Bolingbroke's thoughts on a limited monarchy, a balanced and mixed government, the danger of corruption and of a despotic ministry, the domination of financiers and the curse of a massive debt. These were not to be forgotten as France hurtled along its irreversible path to the Revolution. In America, the new land of freedom, Bolingbroke was very popular, with Jefferson and John Adams in the forefront of his admirers.[80]

Bolingbroke's reputation appeared to recover in the nineteenth century when the passage of time permitted his work to be examined more objectively. English statesmen of Tory sympathies such as Disraeli saw in him a politician who had attempted to implement a new Tory philosophy, although, as Dickinson has well pointed out, it was by no means a coherent political system.[81] Writers such as Goldsmith (who edited his works) felt an evident sympathy with the man, seeing in his tragic destiny only the hand of fate, though others such as Walter Scott could never forgive the posthumous publication of his heretical philosophy. Critics, understandably, have been unable to agree. Cooke, Hassall, Harrop, MacKnight, and Churton Collins were able to give a fairly impartial analysis of his achievement, while John Hunt and Leslie Stephen could not forgive his attacks on orthodox Christianity. In France, at the turn of the century, he gradually received proper recognition as a humanist scholar, a philosophe, and a deist who was anxious to establish a benevolent moral order independent of the trappings of religious dogmatism. Such was the view of Saint-Lambert in his Oeuvres philosophiques.[82] Since there were no further translations of Bolingbroke's works in the century, there was little mention of him in the press. As in England, critics tended to be divided in their scholarly works. Hippolyte Taine who had treated Chesterfield so harshly and deigned only to mention Walpole's name, was more venomous still in dismissing Bolingbroke (whom he ranked with Marlborough) as a traitor, a scoundrel, a trafficker of consciences, and one of the worst roués of the age; with Collins, Tindal and Chesterfield he scorned Christianity as well as concepts of honor and justice.[83] Other critics such as Ludovic Carrau and Desnoiresterres deal with Bolingbroke in the Voltaire-Bolingbroke context and appear to take it for

granted that Voltaire was a disciple of Bolingbroke,
owing to him more than to any other his philosophical
training.[84]   Frequent are the references to his
deistic thought in writers such as Edouard Sayous.[85]

It is Rémusat however who, in his work
L'Angleterre au Dix-huitième siècle, 1856, writes the
most   comprehensive   and   accurate   account   of
Bolingbroke's life and writings.   While deploring his
overweening pride and unbridled passions and agreeing
with other critics that these vices harmed him as an
influential writer ('Sa vie ne recommandait pas sa
doctrine'), he was surprised to find that his
philosophical writings exceeded his expectations - 'En
les lisant nous les avons trouvés supérieurs à notre
attente'.   Without being 'des chefs-d'oeuvre' they
possessed real merit.   The least remarkable were those
dealing with foreign affairs, while the Idea of a
Patriot King, though brilliantly written, was quite
impractical since limitless power would lead to
anarchy, and political liberty could not exist without
political parties.   The Remarks on the History of
England seemd to be his favorite:

On trouvera dans cette composition la suite et
l'unité, l'intelligence de l'histoire, une idée
générale largement développée, une fierté de
langage qui plaît.

Finally, Rémusat accords Bolingbroke a significant
role in shaping the ideas of both Voltaire and
Montesquieu.[86]   His work had been facilitated by the
popularity of General Grimoard's fine edition of
Bolingbroke's correspondence from 1710 to 1736
published earlier in the century (Lettres historiques,
politiques, philosophiques et particulières. . .,
1808) which did much to enhance his influence in
France.   Of the great nineteenth century critics --
Faguet, Brunetière and Sainte-Beuve -- only the latter
has comments on Bolingbroke.   He is praised for his
eloquence and his role in shaping the thought of
French writers (Duclos in particular), but was not
nearly as important in the critic's view as
Chesterfield and Franklin (to whom he devoted
Lundis)[87].   Rathery redeems this lapse however in his
excellent account of the social and intellectual
relations between France and England published in the
Revue contemporaine of 1855 and 1856.   He laments
Bolingbroke's loss of prestige in France, and insists
that his influence on writers such as Voltaire and

Duclos, and on politicians such as Torcy and Fleury, not counting the Pretender himself, was very significant. His brilliant and solid qualities and his plain common sense were evidenced in his works sections of which Rathery reproduces.[88] Caro stresses Bolingbroke's role in the formation of Montesquieu's thought,[89] while Babeau praises Bolingbroke (with Chesterfield) for their contribution in extolling France before the world as being the best school of breeding and elegant writing.[90] Philarète Chasles, often a hostile critic of English deists because of his religious fervor, refers to the extraordinary dynamism of Bolingbroke and his mesmeric influence on other writers such as Chesterfield.[91] In his work on Suard, Garat finds in Bolingbroke 'cette universalité de vues qui en faisait un citoyen du monde autant que de l'Angleterre,' and agrees with Saint-Lambert that he loved France and was in turn loved and respected by the French.[92]

At the turn of the century, Walter Sichel produced his highly eulogistic though somewhat inaccurate and uncritical work on Bolingbroke and his times. With the aid of unpublished letters, he attempted to rehabilitate his idol's reputation as a politician and a philosopher, so badly damaged by the efforts of critics such as Walter Scott and Leslie Stephen. Ironically, and despite Arthur Hassall's endorsement of his views a little later, he did more harm than good, and John Morley's verdict of Bolingbroke as a charlatan appeared not to be invalidated.[93] To Winston Churchill he was an unprincipled miscreant adventurer, the natural reaction of a descendant of the Duke of Marlborough,[94] while D.G. James, in his Life of Reason, delivered a devastating attack on Bolingbroke as a philosopher. It would seem that Burke, whose unfortunate remark on Bolingbroke's boring style overshadowed his more judicious observation on the latter's exemplary and enlightened political philosophy based on reason, had influenced writers like G.D.H. Cole, C.G. Robertson and Carlton Hayes to the point of denying Bolingbroke an important place in the political and philosophical world of his age. Harold Laski appeared so repelled by Bolingbroke's weaknesses of character that he damned him as a serious scholar. Naturally, political partisanship has been a major factor in Bolingbrokian criticism, since he was first and foremost a pillar of the English Tory tradition. Most other critics take the middle road, documenting his weaknesses and his strengths more carefully -- writers such as Strachey,

Butterfield, Jackman, Hart, Mansfield, Harkness, Gosse and Wade. Some, such as Tallentyre and Torrey concentrate on specific aspects of his influence in France (his relations with Voltaire), while others again have stressed what they consider his most important contribution to human thought -- his historical writings. Trevelyan set the tone in the thirties by declaring certain pages of Bolingbroke's letters on history astonishing and illuminating, written as they were before the dawn of modern historical study.[95] In his footsteps, historians such as Kramnick, Nadel, Brumfitt, Briggs, Namier, Pocock and Plumb have evaluated this contribution more minutely. Kramnick's assessment of Bolingbroke as a reactionary conservative who defended the old order and the financial innovations of the early eighteenth century, a cross between a traditionalist and an enlightened philosopher, seems to be eminently judicious.[96] Dennis Fletcher, following on Hurn's study, has, as we have seen, examined the intellectual relations of Bolingbroke with France, while scholars such as Giles Barber, H.T. Dickinson, Robert Shackleton, René Wellek, Brean Hammond, J.H. Grainger and Simon Varey have shown that Bolingbroke was in fact a political force to be reckoned with in his own times and is an influence still to be felt in the contemporary age. As a writer of English prose, a number of critics such as Churton Collins, A.C. Ward, Oliver Elton, Bonamy Dobrée, and T.S. Eliot considered Bolingbroke a master with a permanent influence on his successors.

A parallel re-evaluation of Bolingbroke has been noticeable in French studies since Sichel's work renewed interest in the man of mercury. Inspired by this publication, Joseph Dedieu wrote his excellent study on the English sources of Montesquieu's Esprit des Lois where Bolingbroke is given a major role in the genesis of the work; it was this comparative aspect of Bolingbrokian influence that occupied the minds and pens of succeeding French scholars such as Gustave Lanson, Lucien Foulet, Georges Ascoli, Gabriel Bonno, Emile Audra, Henri Sée, Edouard Sonet, Paul Baratier, Louis Cazamian, Charles Dédéyan and André-Michel Rousseau. The meticulous scholarship of Lanson, Foulet, Sonet and Pomeau bore its fruits in attacking the question of the Voltaire-Bolingbroke relationship. Carefully avoiding the twin reefs of doubt and certainty, they give a measured assessment of this influence in which more recent critics such as

Dédéyan and Rousseau see little to change. All agree that, despite his personal faults and weaknesses as a philosopher, he was of paramount importance in shaping Voltaire's ideas, introducing him to the rich literature of England and inculcating in his receptive mind a knowledge of and fascination for the English political system. Further, his many sojourns in France, his contacts in the highest French spheres, his dynamic personality and glittering eloquence made his retreat at La Source a haven for philosophical speculation, a cosmopolitan forum for the exchange of French and English opinions on all the practical issues of the day in both countries. And this was carried out in a civilized, charming and friendly atmosphere which did much to draw the two nations into an Entente Cordiale that has continued to our day to have a lasting effect on world politics. Rigorous and profound philosophers neither were, though Bolingbroke, and through him Voltaire, had studied Bacon, Locke and Newton, while Pouilly had drawn them both into the great whirlpool of the Cartesian-Newtonian controversy and the metaphysical discussions which further stimulated their own inquisitive and active minds. Interest on both sides of the Channel continues unabated, and once we have a definitive edition of Bolingbroke's works and correspondence, this interest will only be heightened.[97]

NOTES

PART I

1   A French friend of Trumbull's, Michel Le Vassor, alleged author of Les Soupirs de la France esclave (also attributed to Jurieu), was proclaiming the virtues of a constitutional monarchy in France at this time, and it is possible that he and Bolingbroke had some interesting discussions on this topic.

2   Fletcher 3, 9.

3   Daniels, 120, 128-9, and passim.

4   Downshire MSS, Vol. I, Pt.II (Letter to Trumbull, June 9, 1699).

5   e.g. The Spectator, No.305, Feb. 19, 1712; and The Craftsman, No.170, Aug. 30, 1729.

6   According to Grimoard, Bolingbroke was 'reçu en France comme un ange de paix', and people rose in their seats whenever he appeared in public. Bolingbroke 3, II, 71.   Fletcher reports that Bolingbroke attended two banquets, one given by the Duc de Beauvilliers which turned into a drinking orgy, and a second hosted by the Duc de Noailles who presided over a society of libertins that met regularly in the Louvre.   No reference, however, is given.   Fletcher 3, 25.

7   Bolingbroke 3, II, 183, 235.   The good ladies apparently had learned to drink a toast to Bolingbroke and Oxford -- 'à Harri et à Robin'.

8   Fletcher mentions the names of Mme de Parabère and Mme de Courcillon, 'grandes mondaines' of the day. Fletcher 3, 24.

9   Bolingbroke 3, II. 147-8, note 1.

10   Hare MSS, (Prior to Bolingbroke, Sept. 9, 1712).

11   Fletcher 3, 24.

12   Dickinson.   In view however of her liaison with Matthew Prior whom Bolingbroke supplanted, and of her connection with the Abbé Dubois, the French minister who supported Hanover, the possibility cannot be ruled

out. Nevertheless, Horatio Walpole's later testimony, written no doubt to discredit his brother's enemy, should be discounted. See Walpole 1, XVIII, 247, note 25, and Sareil, pp. 41-2

13 One could cite the incriminating documents brought back by Prior on March 25, 1715, and secret information from an official source that mentioned the scaffold. These facts, mentioned in the correspondence between Torcy and d'Iberville, the French envoy, appear to be the immediate cause of his flight. See Fieldhouse, 2, 25.

14 Huntington Library, California. Misc. letters LO 12553, Paris, April 17, 1715.

15 H.MSS.C, Stuart MSS i, 361-2.

16 Dickinson 1, 138-42.

17 See Fletcher 3, 29.

18 Bolingbroke 3, II, 433-4, note 2.

19 Bolingbroke 3, II, 431 (Lettre à Mme de Ferriol, Saint-Clair, 3 juin, 1715). He refers to Mme de Tencin as 'la reine votre soeur'.

20 See for e.g. Bolingbroke 3, III, 61 (Lettre à M. d'Argental, janvier, 1721); III, 289 (Lettre à l'Abbé Alary, 20 mai, 1726); III, 275-6 (Lettre à Mme de Ferriol, 28 décembre, 1725).

21 See Swift 1, II, 305 (Arbuthnot to Swift, Dec. 11, 1718).

22 Baratier, Baldensperger, Dickinson.

23 A daughter of Mlle Aïssé, born from her liaison with the chevalier d'Aydie, was placed in a convent at Sens and brought up as Miss Black, Bolingbroke's 'niece'.

24 He left a diamond ring to the Marquis in his will to be 'kept in the remembrance of a family whom I love and honour above all others'. Bolingbroke 6, I, ccxvii.

25 'Il y a peu de têtes si bien ornées, et peu de coeurs si bien placés'. Bolingbroke 3, II, 460 (Lettre à Mme de Ferriol, fév., 1718).

'Beaucoup de probité dans le coeur, beaucoup de politesse dans les manières, forment, avec un grand fonds de savoir, le caractère d'un homme qu'il serait dommage de perdre à vingt-cinq ans.'

Ibid, III, 38 (Lettre à Mme de Ferriol, 5 août, 1719).

26 Alary's wide circle of scholarly friends, such as the Abbé Asselin and the Abbé de Vertot, would no doubt have been recruited in this learned endeavor.

27 Rapin de Thoyras, III, 71-2. Radice, 309-10. Woodbridge, 50-64.

28 Hic ver assiduum, atque alienis mensibus aestas (Eternal spring and summer out of season). Virgil, Georgics, II, 149.

Fallentis semita vitae (The path of an unnoticed life). Horace, Epistles I 18, 103.

29 Voltaire 1, D 135 (Lettre à Thieriot, [4 déc., 1722]). Rapin de Thoyras, XIII, 83-4.

30 Woodbridge, 62.

31 Pope I, II, 221-2 (Bolingbroke to Pope, Feb. 18, 1724).

32 Hammond, 111.

33 See Bolingbroke 3, III, 239.

34 Briggs 1, 517-18.

35 See Hammond, especially Chapter 5.

36 Bonhomme, 181 (Letter from Caylus to Conti, Nov. 13, 1722). Ibid, 204 (Letter from Caylus to Conti, Dec. 1, 1730).

37 Montagu, II, 256 (Letter to Countess Bute, July 20, 1754). Ibid, II, 361 (Letter to Sir J. Stewart, July 19, 1759).

38 Bolingbroke 3, III, 7 (Lettre à Mme de Ferriol, 4 fév., 1719). It is interesting to note that Voltaire, anxious to curry favor with the great, had sent a copy of this tragedy, with a highly sycophantic dedication,

to King George I, and had also read fragments of his
Henri le Grand to Lord Stair who persuaded the King to
send Voltaire a gold medal and a marvellous repeater
watch.

39 Voltaire 1, D 108.

40 He had originally intended to spend only one day,
and to proceed from La Source to Ussé. See Voltaire
1, D 134 (Lettre à Thieriot, c. 1 déc., 1722).

41 Marais, ii, 377 (déc., 1722). In Marais's eyes,
Bolingbroke was 'une intelligence d'élite'.

42 Voltaire 1, D 135 (Lettre à Thieriot, 4 déc.,
1722). Dédéyan puts the date at 1723 (16), and
Fletcher at 1725 (3, 86, note 1.)

43 Dédéyan 2, 16.

44 Morrison, Series II, i. 323. Some authorities
refer to the poem as La Ligue (or Henri le Grand),
others as La Henriade which was the title of the final
version.

45 Rousseau (André-Michel), I, 60.

46 Voltaire 1, D 150.

47 Baldensperger 3, 33-41.

48 Voltaire 1, D 153 (Lettre à Thieriot, c. 10 juin,
1723).

49 Ibid, D 152 (Lettre à la marquise de Bernières, [7
juin], 1723).

50 The following lines are now omitted:

>   "... Et la science de Varron,
>   Bolingbroke,à ma gloire il faut que je publie
>   Que tes soins, pendant le cours
>   De ma triste maladie,
>   Ont daigné marquer mes jours
>   Par le tendre intérêt que tu prends à ma vie..."

51 Voltaire 4, x, 258 (Epître xxv; à M. de Gervasi,
médecin, 1723).

52   Voltaire 1, D 190 (Bolingbroke à Voltaire, 27 juin, 1724).

53   Rousseau (André-Michel), I, 61. Lord Hervey is cited as another example.

54   Burigny, 27. cited by Rousseau (André-Michel), I, 62.

55   Bolingbroke 3, III, 268 (Lettre à Mme de Ferriol, 5 déc., 1725).

56   Pope 1, ii, 222 (Bolingbroke to Pope, Feb. 18, 1724).

57   Ibid, 229 (Letter to Bolingbroke, April 9, 1724).

58   Voltaire 1, D 303 (Lettre à Thieriot, 26 oct., 1726).

59   See for example Bolingbroke 3, III 268-9 (Lettre à Mme de Ferriol, 5 déc., 1725); III 274 (Lettre à Mme de Ferriol, 28 déc., 1725), and Voltaire 1, D 303 (Lettre à Thieriot, 26 oct., 1726).

60   Voltaire wrote a delightful letter to Brinsden in English in the summer of 1728 (Voltaire I, D 338), praising Henrietta for her brilliant mind, her great stock of learning, her wit, and her linguistic talent.

61   Voltaire 1, D 315 (Lettre à Thieriot, 27 mai, 1727).

62   Voltaire 4, XVI, 321 (Histoire de Charles XII - livre septième).

63   Ibid, II, 312.

64   Ibid, XXVI, 548 (Défense de Milord Bolingbroke).

65   Voltaire 4, XXVI, 488 and see Voltaire 1, D 5793 (Lettre à Mme Denis, 28 avril, 1754) and D 5799 (Lettre au comte d'Argental, 2 mai, 1754) for his condemnation of the Mémoires secrets. Neither the plan nor the style, nor the reasons given were satisfactory. They should have remained secret.

66   Voltaire 1, D 492 (Lettre à Thieriot, 26 mai, 1732).

67   Ibid, D 7499 (Lettre à d'Alembert, 6 déc., 1757).

101

68   Ibid, D 8059 (Lettre à Jacques Abram Elie Daniel Clavel de Brenles, c. 20 jan., 1759).

69   Ibid, D 8792 (Lettre au marquis Francesca Albergati Capacelli, 7 mars, 1760).

70   Ibid, D 8764 (Lettre à la marquise du Deffand, 18 fév., [1760]).

71   Ibid, D 15484 (Lettre au comte de Tourelle, 24 fév., [1760]) and Voltaire's Notebooks I (Voltaire 4), LXXXI, 61).

72   Sherlock reports this comment about Bolingbroke made to him when he visited Ferney:

> 'Sa figure était imposante et sa voix aussi; dans ses oeuvres il y a beaucoup de feuilles mais peu de fruits'
>
> 156 (1971 reprint)

73   Voltaire 1, D 5780 (Lettre à Charles Augustin Ferriol, 16 avril, [1754]).

74   Voltaire 4, XXII, 184 (Mélanges: Lettre XXIV - Sur les Académies).

75   Fletcher 3, 92.

76   This debt was in part paid by Bolingbroke in the Craftsman 'when he referred to Boulainvillier's Gothicism, or commented favorably upon the political and gallican aspirations of the Parlements'. Kramnick, 16.

77   Janet, 125. The italics are mine.

78   For fuller information on the Entresol, see the editions of d'Argenson's Mémoires by Janet and Rathery, the Discours de réception of Lanier, and the works of Briggs 2, and Dédéyan 1, all listed in the bibliography.

79   'a little lower than the angels.' Swift 1, III, 107 (Pope to Swift, Oct. 15, 1725) and see II, 470 (Arbuthnot to Swift, Nov. 7, 1723) where Arbuthnot noted an improvement even in his manners after the brief 1723 visit.

80   See Dickinson 1, 240-2 and Fletcher 3, 100-4.

81 Fletcher 3, 104-5.

82 See Arch. W. Epist. 11, f.225 (Lettre de Courayer
à Wake, 16 jan., 1726), and Préclin, 96.

83 See Coxe, II, 333 (Bolingbroke to Wyndham, Nov.
29, 1735).

84 The young Earl of Huntingdon seemed his particular
favorite, and many of his philosophical views can be
found in this correspondence.   He was also
instrumental in assisting Chesterfield's son Philip
Stanhope to make his way in French society.

85 See Fletcher 3, 110-12.

86 Ibid, 112-14.

NOTES

PART II

1   See Bolingbroke 3, III, 163 (Lettre à Alary, 2
avril, 1722).

2   Bolingbroke 7, II, 467 (The substance of some
letters to M. de Pouilly).

3   Fletcher 1, 29-46.

4   Bolingbroke 3, III, 239 (Lettre à Alary, juin,
1724).

5   Pope 1, I, 220 (Bolingbroke to Pope, Feb. 18,
1724).

6   Malebranche was 'a fine genius wrought up to a
degree of madness by metaphysical speculation and
hypothetical enthusiasm'. Bolingbroke 6, V, 261.
Gassendi was praised for his notion of the sense
origin of ideas and for his objection to the idealism
of Descartes. Ibid, V, 136-7, also VI, 159.

7   Bolingbroke 7, II, 464. Also II, 462, 465, 493,
504.

8   Saint Paul was guilty of much distortion, adding
elements from pagan religions.

9   Bolingbroke 6, VI, 455-6.

10 Ibid, VII, 512.

11 Ibid, VIII, 180-1.

12 To Fontenelle, le bonheur or happiness, was a
state or a situation of mind, different from le
plaisir which was merely a transient though agreeable
feeling.

13 The Rémond brothers, Saint-Mard and le Grec, and
the Marquis de Lassay could be cited in this
connection.

14 Bolingbroke believed that we could never know the
real nature of any substance - we simply had an idea
of objects from personal experience. Thus, he
bestrides both the fields (often contradictory) of

empiricism and relativity. This criticism of pure reason was propounded before that of Kant who was born in 1724. Voltaire was rather a non-relativist.

15 Hurn, 44.

16 Bolingbroke 7, II, 174-94.

17 Rousseau (André-Michel), III, 821.

18 Fletcher 3, 46.

19 Ibid, 61 and note 1.

20 Ibid, 45.

21 Morrison, Series II, I, 316 / cited by Hammond, 34 and 168.

22 See Fletcher 3, 171-2.

23 Pocock 1, 248.

24 Universal Magazine (1794), xciv, 427 (Dodington to Gregory Sharpe, April 24, 1752) '... the Englishman is by far the greater man and the greater scholar' / cited by Rousseau (André-Michel), III, 822, note 201.

25 Journal britannique (1753), X, 38-9.

26 Rousseau (André-Michel), III, 823.

27 Wade 2, 472.

28 Brumfitt 2, 165.

29 Bolingbroke 7, II, 25.

30 Hammond, 127.

31 Hill, 210.

32 Dickinson 1, 304.

33 See Fletcher 3, 191-205.

34 Early in life he had highly praised Roman government, contrasting it with the anarchic society of the Gothic rabble. Later he appeared to revise this opinion somewhat, giving the latter greater credit for wise and prudent laws.

35 Hammond defines Bolingbroke's concept of virtue as 'partly the Christian conception of an innocent and pure soul, and partly the Roman conception of public-spirited action', a concept which he wished to restore 'as a central motive for political conduct'. Hammond, 117.

36 Voltaire 3, Lettre 8, 100.

37 Ibid, Lettre 9, 104.

38 Ibid

39 Ibid, Lettre 10, 120.

40 Ibid, 122.

41 The change in Bolingbroke's political views can be seen when one compares early works such as The Patriot King with later tracts such as Some Reflections on the Present State of the Nation.

42 Usbek refers to the English belief that unlimited power is against all law, while Rica explains that English liberty has risen Phoenix-like from the flames of strife, rebellion, and discord.

43 Cudworth and Clarendon among other authors.

44 See Montesquieu 4, 754, 757 and Mariemont, II 499-502 (Montesquieu to Warburton, July 4, 1752) / cited by Shackleton 1, 55 and note.

45 Dedieu, 282.

46 See Montesquieu 3, I, 12; II, 163, 165, 333; Montesquieu 2, II, 644, 647; Montesquieu 4, 129, 240; Montesquieu 2, III, 1509 (Letter to Warburton, May, 1754); and Fletcher 3, 206-8 and 207 notes 1-5.

47 See note 44, Mariemont, II (Letter to Warburton), and Fletcher F.T.H, 24.

48 Shackleton 1, 152 and note 5.

49 Locke (Essay on Civil Government, Ch.XIII, Section 157).

50 The two debates reported by Montesquieu were 1) the famous speech of Shippen, decrying the use of an army to maintain power, and 2) the acrimonious debate

between Bolingbroke and Walpole on the action of the French government in refortifying the port of Dunkirk in defiance of the Treaty of Utrecht.

51 Machiavelli, 309 (Discorsi, Bk.III, Ch.1) / cited by Shackleton 1, 268.

52 Pocock 2, 480-1. See also Dickinson 1, 202-4, 305-6 and Struck, passim.

53 Shackleton, in his article on the separation of powers, makes a strong argument for the case that Montesquieu did, in fact, derive his famous theory from Bolingbroke. Dickinson's considered opinion is that it was due to his misreading of Bolingbroke.

54 See Montesquieu 3, Vol.II, Section VIII, 346 and Bolingbroke 6, III, 274 (Dissertation upon Parties).

55 See Fletcher 3, 242 and notes 2 & 3, and 243 and notes 1 & 2.

56 Mme Dupin appears to have been a neighbor of Bolingbroke when he was at Chanteloup, being the châtelaine at Chenonceaux.

57 Cazamian, 263.

58 For a detailed discussion of the similarities between The Idea of a Patriot King and Le législateur, see Fletcher 4, 410-18.

59 d'Argenson 2, VI, 466.

60 His Testament politique where he criticizes the French financial system and praises a balanced constitution founded on le génie national of the people is reminiscent of Bolingbroke's Testament politique (French version of the Reflections on the Present State of the Nation).

61 In a letter to Marchmont, he calls England a despicable and despised country. Marchmont, II, 245, March 26, 1741.

62 Chesterfield, II, 450 (No.694) (Letter to Marchmont, April 24, 1741).

63 Fletcher 3, 271-4.

64 Dedieu, 368.

65   Horace Walpole visited d'Holbach's salon seven times during his 1765 visit to France and undoubtedly renewed his friendship in 1769 when d'Holbach visited England.

66   Chesterfield, V, 1802-3 (No.1802) (Lettre à la marquise de Monconseil, 10 jan., 1751).

67   Hervey, I, 16 / cited by Dickinson 1, 313.

68   Walpole, Horace 1, XXV, 6-7 (Letter to Mann, Jan. 13, 1780).

69   Chesterfield, IV, 1462 (No.1677) (Letter to his son, Dec. 23, 1749) / cited by Dickinson 1, 313.

70   Montagu 1, III, 61-5, 76-7.

71   Boswell, I, 246-7.

72   Dickinson 1, 300.

73   See for example Grimm (Kraus reprint), I, 409-10; II, 153-4.   In addition Grimm criticizes his overweening ambition and his radical philosophical views calculated to upset society.   However, he does praise the fire of his style and his bold though judicious reflections in the Mémoires secrets and in the Testament Politique, II, 340, 348.

74   Chesterfield, IV, 1461-2 (No.1677) (Letter to his son, Dec. 23, 1749).

75   See for example Journal de Trévoux, 2415 (Sept.-Dec., 1752) and Fletcher 2, 216.

76   Journal britannique, 38 (jan.-fév., 1753) / cited in full by Fletcher 3, 217.

77   Suard, I, 397.

78   Fréron, VI, 314-32, and see for a detailed account of Bolingbroke's fortunes in France in the eighteenth century, Fletcher 2, 207-32.

79   Mercure de France, II, 113 (octobre, 1768) / cited by Lovering, 197.

80   Adams declared that the Dissertation Upon Parties was a 'jewel', the most profound, correct and perfect

treatise on government in any language. See <u>Kramnick</u>, 262.

81 <u>Dickinson 1</u>, 309. Disraeli's fine homage to Bolingbroke, cited in full by Baratier (357-9), appears in his letter to Lord Lyndhurst of 1835.

82 <u>Saint-Lambert</u>, V, 172 / cited by <u>Fletcher 2</u>, 225. This volume also contains a well-known life of Bolingbroke.

83 <u>Taine</u>, III, 8, 12-13. He was, in fact, 'un professeur d'irréligion', <u>Ibid</u>, 60.

84 See <u>Carrau</u>, 82-91 and <u>Desnoiresterres</u>, I, 245-50 (la jeunesse de Voltaire).

85 See the Bibliography.

86 <u>Rémusat</u>, I, 395-452. It is interesting to note that Rémusat's political ideal was an English-type government, set in a French society.

87 <u>Sainte-Beuve</u>, IX, 255 and VII, 127.

88 <u>Rathery</u>, 95, 99-100.

89 <u>Caro</u>, I, 42.

90 <u>Babeau</u>, 199.

91 <u>Chasles</u>, 911 and see <u>Barrell 1</u>, 28-9, 29, note 16.

92 <u>Garat</u>, II, 83, 86-7.

93 It must be stated in all fairness however, that he did do Bolingbroke justice in stressing his impact on Voltaire's intellectual development.

94 <u>Churchill</u>, IV, 1012. He did however praise Bolingbroke's brilliant oratorical gifts, his elevation of thought and breadth of view, and his mastery of both English and French. II, 623.

95 He refers to the first dozen pages of Letter VI on the Reformation and the rise of national monarchies in his introduction to <u>Bolingbroke's Defence of the Treaty of Utrecht. Being Letters VI-VIII of "The Study and Use of History"</u>. (Cambridge, 1932), vi. Quoted by Fletcher, <u>3</u>, 183.

96 <u>Kramnick</u>, 265.

97 Much of Bolingbroke's correspondence is in private possession and scattered throughout the world; the task of retrieval is thus a formidable one, necessitating amongst other things attendance at auctions, advertisements in newspapers and journals, and personal visits to collectors.

SELECT BIBLIOGRAPHY

PRIMARY SOURCES

I. **MANUSCRIPT SOURCES**

Archives du Ministère des Affaires Etrangères, Quai d'Orsay, Paris.
Correspondence politique: Angleterre, Vols. 358-91, France, Vol. 61.
Mémoires et documents/Fonds divers, Vols. 33-40.

Berkshire Record Office
Downshire MSS (Trumbull Correspondence).

Bibliothèque Nationale, Paris
MSS 10234, 12162, 13634, 15176, 24416, 6363-4, 6489-90.

Bodleian Library, Oxford
Add. MSS A269, D23.
French MSS d.18.

British Museum
Add. MSS 17677 xx-yyy,27732-5, 34196, 34753 (f.31), 35584- 8, 37994, 40787, 49970-1.
Birch MSS 4282-3, 4291.
Egerton MSS 1717, 1959, 2618.
Lansdowne MSS 773
Portland (Harley) papers, loan 29.

Cambridge University Library
Add. MSS 6570, 7093.

Christ Church, Oxford
Arch. W. Epist., Vol.11, f.225.

Harvard University Library
Houghton MSS 51M-176 (6-8).

Henry E. Huntington Library, California
Stowe MSS ST (57-8).
Misc. letters LO 12552-3.

Historical MSS Commission
Bath MSS I, i-ii.
Denbigh MSS V.
Downshire MSS I, i-ii.
Polwarth MSS i, iii, v.
Portland MSS ii-x.

Stuart MSS i-vii.
Townshend MSS.

Norwich and Norfolk Record Office
Hare MSS 6160, 6164.

Petworth House
Egremont MSS (Wyndham family correspondence).

Scottish Record Office
Stair MSS GD.135, Vols. 138-47.

Yale University Library
Osborn Collection (Misc. letters).

II. ORIGINAL SOURCES IN PRINT

Argenson, le marquis d'
1. <u>Considérations sur le gouvernement ancien et présent de la France</u>, Amsterdam, 1764.
2. <u>Journal et Mémoires</u> (éd. E.J.B. Rathery), Paris, 1859-68, 9 vols. (Johnson reprint, London, New York, 1968)
3. <u>Mémoires et journal inédit</u> (éd. P. Janet), Paris, 1857-8, 5 vols.

Berwick, le maréchal de
<u>Mémoires</u> (éd. Michaud et Poujolat), Paris, 1872.

Bibliothèque des Sciences et des Beaux-Arts

Bibliothèque raisonnée

Bolingbroke, Lord
1. <u>Contributions to the Craftsman</u> (ed. S. Varey), Oxford, 1982.
2. <u>Letters and Correspondence</u> (ed. G. Parke), London, 1798, 4 vols.
3. <u>Lettres historiques, politiques, philosophiques et particulières de Henri St. John, Lord Vicomte Bolingbroke depuis 1710 jusqu'en 1736</u> (éd. Grimoard), Paris, 1808, 3 vols.
4. <u>Lettres inédites à Lord Stair</u> (1716-20) (éd. P. Baratier), Trévoux, 1939.
5. <u>Reflections concerning Innate Moral Principles</u> (in French and English), London, 1752.
6. <u>Works</u> (Preface of O. Goldsmith), London, 1809, 8 vols.

114

7. Works (reprint of 1844 edition), London, 1967, 4 vols.

Boswell, James
The Life of Samuel Johnson, London, 1816, 4 vols.

Boulainvilliers, le comte de
Histoire de l'ancien gouvernement de la France, Amsterdam, 1727, 3 vols.

Burigny, Jean Lévesque de
Lettre [...] à M. l'abbé Mercier sur les démêlés de M. de Voltaire avec M. de Saint-Hyacinthe, Londres et Paris, 1780.

Burke, Edmund
Works, London, 1887, 12 vols.

Caylus, le comte de
Souvenirs, Paris, 1805.

Chesterfield, Lord
Letters (ed. B. Dobrée), London, 1932.

Clément, S.
Les cinq années littéraires, Berlin, 1755, 2 vols.

Coxe, William
Memoirs of Horatio, Lord Walpole, London, 1820, 2 vols.

Craftsman
Collected edition, 1731 and 1737, 14 vols.

Disraeli, B.
Vindication of the English Constitution in a letter to a noble and learned friend, London, 1835.

Dodington, Bubb
'Letter to Gregory Sharpe', Universal Magazine, 1794, XCIV.

Fénelon
Oeuvres choisies, Paris, 1920.

Fontenelle
Oeuvres, Paris, 1825.

Fréret, N.
Réponse aux observations sur la chronologie de

M. Newton avec une lettre de M.-- [Conti] au sujet de la dite réponse, Paris, 1726.

Fréron, E.-C.
Lettres sur quelques écrits de ce temps, Paris, 1749- 54, 13 vols.

Gentleman's Magazine

Grimm, Friedrich Melchior, Baron von
Correspondance littéraire, philosophique et critique, (éd. M. Tourneux), Paris, 1877-82, 16 vols.
(Kraus reprint, Paris, 1968)

Hervey, Lord
Memoirs of the reign of George II (ed. R. Sedgwick), London, 1831, 3 vols.

Journal britannique

Journal de Trévoux

Journal des Savants

Locke, John
Two Treatises on Government, London, 1828 (especially - Essay on Civil Government).

Machiavelli
Opere (ed. Riccardo Ricciardi), Milan-Naples, 1958.

Marais, Mathieu
Journal et Mémoires (éd. M. Lescure), Paris, 1863-8, 4 vols.

Marchmont, Earl of
A Selection from the Papers (ed. G.H. Rose), London 1831, 3 vols.

Mariemont, Musée de
Autographes (éd. M. Durry), Paris, 1955, 2 vols.

Maty, M.
'Les Lettres sur l'Histoire de Bolingbroke', Journal britannique, (1753), vol. 10.

Mercure de France

Montagu, Lady Mary Wortley
1. The Complete Letters (ed. R. Halsband), Oxford, 1965-7, 3 vols.
2. Works (6th edition), London, 1812, 2 vols.

Montesquieu
1. Correspondance (éd. Gebelin et Morize), Bordeaux, 1914, 2 vols.
2. Oeuvres complètes (éd. A. Masson), Paris, 1950, 1953, 1955, 3 vols.
3. Pensées et fragments inédits (éd. Baron Gaston de Montesquieu), Bordeaux, 1901, 2 vols.
4. Le Spicilège (éd. A. Masson), Paris, 1944.

Morrison, Alfred
Catalogue of the Collection of Autograph letters and Historical Documents (ed. A.W. Thibaudeau), London, 1883-92, Series I, 6 vols.; 1893-7, Series II, 5 vols.

Pope, Alexander
1. Correspondence (ed. G. Sherburn), Oxford, 1956, 5 vols.
2. The Twickenham edition of the Poems (ed. J. Butt et al.), London, 1939-67, 10 vols.

Pouilly, Lévesque de
1. Dissertation sur l'incertitude de l'histoire des premiers siècles de Rome (lue à l'Académie des Inscriptions, mars, 1723). Recueil de mémoires, dissertations, lettres et autres ouvrages critiques, historiques et littéraires pour servir de supplément aux Mémoires de l'Académie Royale des Sciences et de celle des Inscriptions et Belles-lettres, Vol. 115.
2. La Théorie des sentiments agréables, Paris, 1747.

Rapin, le père René
Instructions pour l'histoire, Paris, 1677.

Rousseau, Jean-Jacques
Oeuvres complètes (éd. Gagnebin et Raymond), Paris, 1961-2, 2 vols.

Saint-Hyacinthe, Thémiseul de
Recueil de divers écrits sur l'Amour, et l'Amitié, la Politesse, la Volupté, les Sentiments Agréables, l'Esprit et le Coeur, Paris, 1736.

Saint-Lambert J.-F., Marquis de
Oeuvres philosophiques, Paris (1801), 5 vols.

Sainte-Beuve, Charles-Augustin
Causeries du Lundi, Paris, 1882-5, 16 vols.

Sherlock, Martin
Letters from an English traveller, London, 1780
(reprinted in New York, 1971).

Silhouette, Etienne de
Testament politique, s.l., 1772.

Spectator

Spence, Joseph
Anecdotes, Observations and Characters of Books and
Men collected from the conversation of Mr. Pope and
other eminent persons of his time (ed. J.M.
Osborn), Oxford, 1966, 2 vols.

Stair, Lord
Annals and Correspondence (ed. J.M. Graham),
Edinburgh, 1875, 2 vols.

Suard, J.B.
Variétés littéraires, Paris, 1768-9.

Swift, Jonathan
1. Correspondence (ed. H. Williams), Oxford 1963-6,
   5 vols.
2. Journal to Stella (ed. H. Williams), Oxford,
   1948, 2 vols.
3. The Prose Works (ed. H. Davis), Oxford, 1939-64,
   13 vols.

Taine, Hippolyte
Histoire de la littérature anglaise, Paris, 1863, 4
vols.

Taylor, Brook
Contemplatio Philosophica (ed. Sir W. Young),
London, 1793.

Thoyras, Rapin de
Histoire d'Angleterre, La Haye, 1749, 15 vols.

Torcy, J.-B.-C., Marquis de
Mémoires, La Haye - Paris, 1756, 3 vols.

Universal Magazine

Voltaire
1. <u>Correspondence</u> (ed. T. Besterman), Oxford, Voltaire Foundation, 1968-77, vols. 85-135 of the <u>Oeuvres complètes</u>.
2. <u>Correspondance (1726-9)</u> (éd. L. Foulet), Paris, 1913.
3. <u>Les lettres philosophiques</u> (éd. G. Lanson), Paris 1909, 2 vols. (Revised Edition A.-M. Rousseau, 1964).
4. <u>Oeuvres complètes</u> (éd. T. Besterman), Oxford, Voltaire Foundation, 1968-

Wake, Archbishop
(see **MANUSCRIPT SOURCES**, Christ Church, Oxford).

Walpole, Horace
1. <u>Correspondence</u> (Yale edition, ed. W.S. Lewis et al.), New Haven, 1937-83, 48 vols.
2. <u>Works</u> (ed. R. Berry), London, 1798.

Warburton, William
<u>Works</u> (ed. R. Hurd), London, 1841, 13 vols.

SECONDARY SOURCES

Ascoli, Georges
'l'Etat d'esprit philosophique de Voltaire avant le séjour en Angleterre', <u>Revue des Cours et Conférences</u>, avril 1924, vol. 25.

Audra, E.
<u>L'Influence française dans l'oeuvre de Pope</u>, Paris, 1931.

Babeau, A.
<u>Les Voyageurs en France</u>, Paris, 1885.

Baillon, Ch. de
<u>Lord Walpole à la cour de France</u>, Paris, 1867.

Baldensperger, F.
1. 'Intellectuels français hors de France', <u>Revue des Cours et Conférences</u>, 1934-5, vols. I and II.
2. 'Une grande Anglaise de France', <u>Etudes d'histoire littéraire</u>, 1939, vol. III (Slatkine reprint, Genève, 1973).
3. 'Voltaire, anglophile avant son séjour d'Angleterre', <u>Revue de littérature comparée</u>, 1929, vol. IX.

Ballantyne, A.
Voltaire's visit to England (1726-9), London, 1893
(Slatkine reprint, Genève, 1970).

Baratier, Paul
Lord Bolingbroke: Ses écrits politiques, Paris, 1939.

Barber, Giles
1. A Bibliography of Bolingbroke, Oxford (B.Litt.
   Thesis), 1963.
2. 'Bolingbroke, Pope, and the Patriot King', The
   Library (1964), XIX.
3. 'Some uncollected authors. Bolingbroke', The Book
   Collector, 1965, XIV.

Barrell, R.A.
1. Chesterfield et la France, Paris, 1968.
2. French Correspondence of Chesterfield, Ottawa,
   1980, 2 vols.
3. Horace Walpole and France, New York, 1978, Vol. I;
   Ottawa, 1979, Vol. II.

Besterman
(See Voltaire, PRIMARY SOURCES).

Bonhomme, H.
Mme de Maintenon et sa famille, Paris, 1863.

Bonno, G.
1. La Constitution britannique devant l'opinion
   française de Montesquieu à Bonaparte, Paris, 1931.
2. La Culture et la Civilisation britannique
   devant l'opinion française au XVIII siècle de la
   paix d'Utrecht aux lettres philosophiques,
   Philadelphia, 1948.

Briggs, E.R.
1. 'L'incrédulité et la pensée anglaise en France au
   début du XVIIIe siècle', Revue d'histoire
   littéraire de la France, 1936.
2. The Political Academies of France in the
   early eighteenth century with special reference to
   the Club de l'Entresol and its founder, Pierre
   Joseph Alary, Cambridge (Univ. thesis), 1931.

Brumfitt, J.H.
1. La Philosophie de l'histoire, SVEC, Genève, 1963,
   Vol. 28.
2. Voltaire: Historian, Oxford, 1958.

Butterfield, Herbert
The Statecraft of Machiavelli, London, 1960.

Carcassonne, E.
Montesquieu et le problème de la constitution
française au XVIIIe siècle, Paris, 1907.

Caro, E.M.
La fin du XVIIIe siècle: Etudes et portraits I,
Paris, 1880.

Carr, J.C.
'Voltaire in England', The Cornhill Magazine, 1882,
Vol. 46.

Carrau, L.
La philosophie religieuse en Angleterre, Paris, 1888.

Cazamian, L.
A History of French Literature, Oxford, 1966.

Chasles, Philarète
'Lord Chesterfield', Revue des deux mondes (15 déc.,
1845), XII.

Churchill, Winston S.
Marlborough: His Life and Times, London, 1933-8, 4
vols. (in 2 books)

Clark, Ruth
Sir William Trumbull in Paris, Cambridge, 1938.

Cole, G.D.H.
Politics and Literature, London, 1929.

Collins, J. Churton
1. Bolingbroke: An historical study, and Voltaire in
   England, London, 1886.
2. Voltaire, Montesquieu and Rousseau in England,
   London, 1908.

Cooke, G.W.
The Memoirs of Lord Bolingbroke, London, 1835, 2 vols.

Coxe, William
(See PRIMARY SOURCES)

Daniels, W.M.
Saint-Evremond en Angleterre, Versailles, 1907.

121

Dédéyan, Charles
1. _Montesquieu et l'Angleterre_, Paris, 1958.
2. _Voltaire et la pensée anglaise_, Paris, 1956.

Dedieu, J.
Montesquieu et la tradition politique anglaise en France, Paris, 1909.

Desnoiresterres, G.
Voltaire et la société au XVIIIe siècle, Paris, 1867-76, 8 vols. (Slatkine reprint, Genève, 1967).

Dickinson, H.T.
1. _Bolingbroke_, London, 1970.
2. 'Henry St. John: a reappraisal of the young Bolingbroke', _Journal of British Studies_ (1968), VII, No.2.
3. 'Bolingbroke's attack on Pope in 1746', _Notes and Queries_ (1969), CCXIV, New Series XVI.
4. 'Bolingbroke and _The Idea of a Patriot King_, 1749', _History Today_ (Jan. 1970), XX.

Dictionary of National Biography (DNB)

Dobrée, Bonamy
English Literature in the early Eighteenth Century, Oxford, 1959.

Eliot, T.S.
The Literature of Politics, London, 1955.

Elton, Oliver
A Survey of English literature 1730-1789, London, 1928, 2 vols.

Fieldhouse, H.N.
'Bolingbroke's share in the Jacobite intrigue of 1710-14', _English Historical Review_, July, 1937, lii.

Fletcher, Dennis, J.
1. _Bolingbroke and the diffusion of Newtonianism in France_, SVEC, 1967, vol. 53.
2. _The Fortunes of Bolingbroke in France in the Eighteenth Century_, SVEC, 1966, vol. 47.
3. _The Intellectual Relations of Lord Bolingbroke with France_, Wales (M.A. Thesis), 1953.
4. '_Le législateur_ and the Patriot King: A case of intellectual kinship', _Comparative Literature Studies_ (1969), VI.

Fletcher, F.T.H.
Montesquieu and English Politics, London, 1939.

Foulet, Lucien
1. (éd) La Correspondance de Voltaire de 1726-29 (see
   Voltaire 2, PRIMARY SOURCES).
2. 'Voltaire en Angleterre', Revue d'histoire
   littéraire de la France, 1908, XV.
3. 'Le voyage de Voltaire en Angleterre', Revue
   d'histoire littéraire de la France, 1906, XIII.

Garat, D.J.
Mémoires historiques sur le XVIIIe siècle et sur M.
Suard, Paris, 1820, 2 vols.

Genet, Abbé
Etude sur la vie, l'administration et les travaux
littéraires de Louis-Jean Lévesque de Pouilly, Travaux
de l'académie nationale de Reims, 1878-9, Vol. 66.

Gooch, G.P.
French profiles: prophets and pioneers, London, 1961.

Grimoard
(See Bolingbroke, PRIMARY SOURCES).

Gunny, Ahmad
Voltaire and English literature, SVEC, 1977, Vol. 177.

Gwynn, W.B.
The Meaning of the Separation of Powers, New Orleans,
1965.

Hammond, Brean S.
Pope and Bolingbroke, Columbia, 1984.

Horaszti, Zoltan
John Adams and Prophets of Progress, Cambridge, Mass.,
1952.

Harkness, Douglas
Bolingbroke. The Man and his Career, London, 1957.

Harpe, J. de la
Le Journal des Savants et l'Angleterre (1702-89), U.
of California Pub. in Mod.Phil., Vol. 20, no.6.

Harris, R.W.
Reason and Nature in the Eighteenth Century, London,
1968.

Harrop, Robert
Bolingbroke: A political study and criticism, London,
1884.

Hart, Jeffrey
Viscount Bolingbroke. Tory humanist, London, 1965.

Hassall, Arthur
A life of Viscount Bolingbroke, Oxford, 1915.

Hazard, Paul
1. La crise de la conscience européenne, Paris, 1935,
   3 vols.
2. La Pensée européenne au XVIIIe siécle, Paris, 1946,
   3 vols.

Henry, Nannerl O.
(See Keohane)

Hill, B.W.
The growth of political parties (1689-1742), London,
1976.

Hunter, A.C.
Suard J.B.A. -- un introducteur de la littérature
anglaise en France, Paris, 1925.

Hurn, A.S.
Voltaire et Bolingbroke, Paris, 1915.

Jackman, S.W.
Man of Mercury, London, 1965.

James, D.G.
The Life of Reason, London, 1949.

Janet, Paul
Une académie politique sous le cardinal de Fleury de
1724 à 1731, Paris, Séances et travaux de l'Académie
des sciences morales et politiques, 1865, vol. 74.

Keohane, Nannerl O. (née Henry)
1. Democratic Monarchy: The political theory of the
   Marquis d'Argenson, Yale (Ph.D. Thesis), 1968.
2. Philosophy and the State in France, Princeton,
   1980.

Koyré, A.
Newtonian Studies, London, 1965.

Kramnick, Isaac
Bolingbroke and his Circle, Cambridge, Harvard, 1968.

Lanier, L.
Le Club de l'Entresol (1723-31), Amiens, Mémoires de l'Académie, 1880, 6, series 3.

Lanson, Gustave
1. (éd.) Les Lettres philosophiques, (see Voltaire 3, PRIMARY SOURCES).
2. 'Voltaire et les lettres philosophiques', Revue de Paris, Aug. 1908.

Legouis et Cazamian
Histoire de la littérature anglaise, Paris, 1924.

Leland, J.
A view of the principal deistic writers, London, 1808, 2 vols.

Lenoir, Raymond
Les Historiens de l'esprit humain, Paris, 1926 (Chapitre sur Bolingbroke).

Lovering, Stella
L'activité intellectuelle de l'Angleterre d'après l'ancien 'Mercure de France' (1672-1778), Paris, 1930.

MacKnight, Thomas
Life of Bolingbroke, London, 1863.

Mansfield, Harvey C.
Statesmanship and Party Government, Chicago, 1965.

Mason, Haydn T.
1. Pierre Bayle and Voltaire, Oxford, 1963.
2. Voltaire, London, 1975.
3. Voltaire. A Biography, Baltimore, 1981.

Masson, P.M.
Madame de Tencin, Paris, 1909.

Merrill, W.M.
From Stateman to Philosopher. A study in Bolingbroke's Deism, New York, 1949.

Morley, John
Walpole [Sir Robert], London, 1889.

Mornet, D.
1. Les origines intellectuelles de la Révolution française Paris, 1933.
2. La Pensée française au XVIIIe siècle, Paris, 1929.

Nadel, George, H.
1. 'New light on Bolingbroke's Letters on History', Journal of the History of Ideas, 1962, Vol. 23.
2. 'Philosophy of History before Historicism', Studies in the Philosophy of History (ed. Nadel), New York, 1965.

Nelson, Elizabeth
Chesterfield and Voltaire, U. of Maryland (Ph.D. Thesis), 1965.

Nichols, John
Literary anecdotes of the Eighteenth Century, London, 1812-16, 9 vols.

Petrie, Charles
Bolingbroke, London, 1937.

Plumb, J.H.
1. The Growth of Political Stability in England, London, 1967.
2. Sir Robert Walpole, London, 1956-60, 2 vols.

Pocock, J.G.A.
1. The Ancient Constitution and the Feudal Law: A study of English historical thought in the Seventeenth Century, Cambridge, 1957.
2. The Machiavellian Moment, Princeton, 1975.

Pomeau, René
1. Etat présent des études voltairiennes, SVEC, Genève, 1955, Vol. 1.
2. La Religion de Voltaire, Paris, 1956.
3. 'Voltaire en Angleterre', Annales Faculté Lettres, Toulouse, 1955, Vol. 3.

Préclin, E.
L'Union des Eglises gallicane et anglicane, Paris, 1928.

Quarterly Review
Lord Bolingbroke in Exile, 1856, Vol. 151 (Jan.-Apr.).

Radice, Sheila
'Bolingbroke in France', Notes and Queries, 1939, Vol. 177.

Rathery, E.J.B.
'Des Relations sociales et intellectuelles entre la France et l'Angleterre depuis la conquête des Normands jusqu'à la Révolution française', Revue contemporaine, 1855-6.

Rémusat, Charles de
L'Angleterre au XVIIIe siècle, études et portraits, Paris, 1865, 2 vols.

Reynald, Hermile
'Les Correspondants de Voltaire', Revue des cours littéraires, juillet, 1868.

Robertson, C.G.
Bolingbroke, London, 1947.

Robertson, J.M.
Bolingbroke and Walpole, London, 1919.

Rousseau, André-Michel
L'Angleterre et Voltaire, SVEC, Genève, 1976, Vols. 145-7.

Sareil, Jean
Les Tencin, Genève, 1969.

Sayous, E.
Les déistes anglais et le christianisme depuis Toland jusqu'à Chubb (1696-1738), Paris, 1882.

Sée, Henri
1. 'Les idées politiques de Voltaire', Revue historique, 1908.
2. Les idées politiques en France au XVIIIe siècle, Paris, 1920.

Shackleton, Robert
1. Montesquieu, a critical biography, Oxford, 1961.
2. 'Montesquieu, Bolingbroke, and the Separation of Powers', French Studies, 1949, Vol. 3.

Sichel, Walter
Bolingbroke and his Times, London, 1901-2 (reprint, New York, 1968), 2 vols.

Simon, Renée
Un révolté du XVIIIe siècle: Henry de Boulainviller, Garches, 1948.

Skinner, Quentin
'The Principles and Practice of Opposition: The Case of Bolingbroke versus Walpole', Historical Perspectives: Studies in English Thought and Society in Honour of J.H. Plumb, edited by Neil McKendrick, 1974.

Sonet, Edouard
Voltaire et l'influence anglaise, Rennes, 1926.

Stephen, Leslie
1. English thought in the Eighteenth Century, London, 1881, (reprint, New York, 1949), 2 vols.
2. English literature and life in the Eighteenth Century, London, 1904.

Strachey, Lytton
'Voltaire and England', Books and Characters, London, 1922.

Struck, W.
Montesquieu als Politiker, Berlin, 1933.

Tallentyre, S.G.
'The English friends of Voltaire', Cornhill Magazine, Aug. 1904, Vol. 17.

Texte, J.
J.J. Rousseau et le cosmopolitisme littéraire, Paris, 1895.

Torrey, N.L.
1. 'Bolingbroke and Voltaire - A fictitious influence', PMLA, 1927, Vol. 42.
2. Voltaire and the English Deists, New Haven, 1930.
3. 'Voltaire's English Notebooks', Modern Philology, 1928- 9.

Trevelyan, G.M.
England under Queen Anne, London, 1930-4, 3 vols.

Trevor-Roper, H.H.
The Historical philosophy of the Enlightenment, SVEC, Genève, 1963, Vols. 24-7.

Van Roosbroeck, L.
'Voltaire, or the abbé Alary?', Modern Language Notes, Jan., 1924.

Varey, Simon
Henry St. John, Viscount Bolingbroke, Boston, 1984.

Vaucher, P.
1. La Crise du ministère Walpole en 1733-4, Paris, 1924.
2. Robert Walpole et la politique de Fleury (1731-42), Paris, 1924.

Villemain, A.F.
1. 'Voltaire in England', Notes and Queries, Series 11, 1914, Vol. 10 (July-November).
2. 'Voltaire in London', Notes and Queries, Series 5, 1878, Vol. 10 (June-July); Series 6, 1884, Vol 9 (April).

Vroil, Jules de
'Etude historique sur Louis-Jean Lévesque de Pouilly', Revue de Champagne et de Brie, 1877, Vol. 3 (jan. - juin).

Wade, Ira
1. The clandestine organisation and diffusion of philosophic ideas in France from 1700 to 1750, New York, 1967.
2. The intellectual development of Voltaire, Princeton, 1969.
3. Voltaire and Mme du Châtelet, Princeton, 1941.

Ward, Alfred C. English Literature, London, 1958.

Williams, Basil
Stanhope, Oxford, 1932.

Williams, David
Voltaire, literary critic, SVEC, Genève, 1966, Vol. 48.

Woodbridge, Kenneth
'Bolingbroke's château of La Source', Garden History 4 (Autumn 1976), 50-64.

INDEX OF PERSONS

131

- D -

- E -

135

Pocock, John Greville Agard   59, 79, 94
Polybius   74
Pomeau, René   94
Pont-de-Veyle, Antoine de Ferriol, Comte de   10, 15
Pope, Alexander   14, 15, 16, 18, 19, 23, 24-5, 27, 29,
    32, 34, 37, 46, 50, 51, 56, 73, 78, 83, 87
Pouilly (see Lévesque de Pouilly)
Pretender, the Old (see Stuart, James Edward)
Price, Cecil   1
Prior, Matthew   7, 71, 97, 98
Ptolemy   39, 44
Pulteney, William, Earl of Bath   74
Pye, Samuel   90

- R -

Rabelais, François   44
Racine, Jean   24
Radice, Sheila   14
Ramsay, Andrew Michael, Chevalier de   30, 31, 36, 68
Rapin de Thoyras, Paul de   2, 4, 14, 17, 32, 57, 70,
    75, 83
Rapin, le père René   57
Rathery, Edme Jacques Benoît   92, 93, 102
Rémond de Montmort, Pierre 15, 17
Rémond de Saint-Mard, Toussaint (de) 17, 105
Rémond le Grec, Nicolas-François 17, 105
Rémusat, Charles, Comte de   92, 110
Richelieu, Armand de Vignerot du Plessis, Maréchal de
    22
Richelieu, Armand Emmanuel du Plessis, Cardinal de
    29, 69
Richmond, Charles Lennox, 2nd Duke of   33, 34, 35, 36
Richmond, Duchess of   34
Robertson, Sir Charles Grant   93
Rohan, Chevalier de   19
Rousseau, André-Michel   vii, 21, 23, 25, 54, 60, 94,
    95
Rousseau, Jean-Jacques   31, 81-2
Ruffhead, Owen   25

- S -

Saint-Evremond, Charles de Marguetel de Saint-Denis de
    5, 41, 53, 56
Saint-Hyacinthe, Thémiseul de (Hyacinthe Cordonnier)
    4, 6, 16, 32-3, 45

Tindal, Matthew 41, 91
Toland, John 41
Torcy, Jean-Baptiste Colbert, Marquis de 3, 7, 9, 11, 29, 93, 98
Torcy, Marquise de 7, 11
Torrey, Norman 46, 94
Townshend, Charles, 2nd Viscount 72
Trevelyan, George Macaulay 94
Trumbull, Sir William 4, 5, 7
Turgot, Anne Robert Jacques 61

- V -

Varey, Simon vii, 1, 32, 94
Varro, Marcus Terentius 100
Vertot, René Aubert, Abbé de 13, 55, 67, 68, 99
Vico, Giambattista 59
Villars-Brancas, Duc de 13
Villette, Marie-Claire de Marcilly, Marquise de 12, 14, 17, 18, 21, 25, 33, 34, 46, 73
Virgil 20
Volar, Mme de 12
Voltaire, François-Marie Arouet de
    vii, 2, 5, 12, 14, 15, 16, 18, 19-28, 31, 32, 35, 39, 45, 46-52, 54, 55, 56, 57, 58-61, 68, 69, 70-2, 76, 82, 83, 89, 90, 91-2, 94, 95, 99-100, 101, 102, 106, 110

- W -

Wade, Ira 60, 94
Waldegrave, James, 1st Earl 34, 72
Walpole, Horace, 4th Earl of Orford
    vii, 1, 2, 4, 5, 13, 17, 25, 28, 68, 85, 88, 91, 109
Walpole, Horatio, 1st Baron Walpole of Wolterton 15, 30, 72, 80, 98
Walpole, Sir Robert, 1st Earl of Orford 13, 25, 32, 33, 58, 62, 63, 65, 66, 68, 80, 85, 88, 98, 108
Warburton, William 73, 88
Ward, Alfred Charles 94
Wellek, René 94
Wharton, Angelica Magdalena 3
Winchcombe, Frances (1st Lady Bolingbroke) 6
Wollaston, William 41
Woodbridge, Kenneth 14

ABOUT THE AUTHOR

REX A. BARRELL is Professor Emeritus of French Language and Literature at the University of Guelph, Guelph, Ontario, CANADA.

He received his B.A. (1941), B.Sc. and M.A. (1944) from the University of Canterbury, Christchurch, New Zealand, where he was born, his A.T.C.L. and L.T.C.L. diplomas from London, his Certificat d'études pratiques from the University of Paris in 1949, and his Doctorat (magna cum laude) from the same University in 1951.

The recipient of numerous awards including a Nuffield Fellowship, a Carnegie Travel Grant, two Canada Council Leave Fellowships, a Fellowship of the Intercontinental Biographical Association, and several Canada Council research and publication grants, he has written eight books and several articles in the fields of Comparative Literature and Philology, and Anglo-French relations in the Eighteenth Century.

The present study completes a trilogy, Chesterfield and Horace Walpole having already been published in 1968 and 1978-79 respectively. He has also completed an edition of <u>Musset et Shakespeare</u>, shortly to appear with Peter Lang (New York, Bern, Frankfort/M, Paris), and a study on <u>Shaftesbury and 'le refuge français'--Correspondence</u>, which is to be published this year by the Edwin Mellen Press.